London

GW00492622

COLLINS
Glasgow & London

Hampton Court

First published 1990
Copyright © William Collins Sons & Company Limited
Published by William Collins Sons & Company Limited
Printed in Hong Kong
ISBN 0 00 435778-7

HOW TO USE THIS BOOK

Your Collins Traveller Guide will help you find your way around your chosen destination quickly and easily. It is colour-coded for easy reference:

The blue-coded 'topic' section answers the question 'I would like to see or do something; where do I go and what do I see when I get there?' A simple, clear layout provides an alphabetical list of activities and events, offers you a selection of each, tells you how to get there, what it will cost, when it is open and what to expect. Each topic in the list has its own simplified map, showing the position of each item and the nearest landmark or transport access, for instant orientation. Whether your interest is Architecture or Sport you can find all the information you need quickly and simply. Where major resorts within an area require in-depth treatment, they follow the main topics section in alphabetical order.

The red-coded section is a lively and informative gazetteer. In one alphabetical list you can find essential facts about the main places and cultural items - 'What is La Bastille?', 'Who was Michelangelo?' - as well as practical and invaluable travel information. It covers everything you need to know to help you enjoy yourself and get the most out of your time away, from Accommodation through Babysitters, Car Hire, Food, Health, Money, Newspapers, Taxis and Telephones to Zoos.

Cross-references: Type in small capitals - **CHURCHES** - tells you that more information on an item is available within the topic on churches. A-Z in bold - **A-Z** - tells you that more information is available on an item within the gazetteer. Simply look under the appropriate heading. A name in bold - **Holy Cathedral** - also tells you that more information on an item is available in the gazetteer under that particular heading.

Packed full of information and easy to use - you'll always know where you are with your Collins Traveller Guide!

Photographs by **Michael Dent**
Cover picture by **Travel Photo International**

INTRODUCTION

Attached to the downstream side of Charing Cross Railway Bridge is a narrow and fragile-seeming walkway, known as the Hungerford Footbridge, which enables the pedestrian to cross the Thames from Victoria Embankment to the South Bank. Use the walkway not too late on a fine night, stop halfway across to gaze downriver, ignore as best you can the shivering of the ground beneath your feet as trains clank by behind you, and you will be rewarded as magnificent a view as any city in the world has to offer and one that seems to encapsulate the special quality of London. In the light-studded panorama laid out before you past and present splendidly co-exist, the successive historical selves of the nation's capital as powerful a presence as its thrusting contemporary self.

Here the Thames, as though gathering itself for its final surge into the sea 50 miles on, alters course from northwards to eastwards, shrinking your view of its south bank but disclosing its north bank in a long concave swathe. To your right, then, you have the undilutedly modern, and at night very impressive, spectacle of the South Bank Centre - the glass river frontage of the Royal Festival Hall ablaze with light immediately to your right, further on the shadowy geometric shapes of the Queen Elizabeth Hall and the Hayward Gallery with the London Weekend Television towerblock rearing up busily bright beyond. To your left and ahead of you, curving round with the river to the limit of your vision, is a much more complex cityscape, rich with architectural variety.

Distant high-rise buildings - Telecom Tower, Centrepoint, the Barbican towers, the Nat-West tower - glow against the night sky, proclaiming London as a city of the late twentieth century. Nearer at hand, or made to seem near by floodlighting, landmarks of a different ilk and different again from each other - Shell-Mex House of the 1930s, Somerset House of the late 18thC, the early 18thC steeple of St Bride's, 17thC St Paul's - give another picture of London. This London is a city which has accrued, century by century, decade by decade. The two notions are not incompatible. London has always readily renewed itself but never so as to wipe out all trace of the old. Each period of the city's history - Roman, Saxon, Norman, Medieval, Tudor, Elizabethan, Stuart, Georgian, Regency, Victorian - is to some degree still manifest alongside the constructions of the 20thC, the later periods very substantially.

For resident and visitor alike, this is an unfailing pleasure, both a stimulant of curiosity and a gratification.

If, from the vantage point of Hungerford Footbridge, you look beyond Waterloo Bridge to the north side of the Thames, you can see where London began its existence. In AD 43 the legions of Claudius established on the raised ground of Cornhill a settlement which they were to call Londinium. 80 years on the settlement had spread to neighbouring Ludgate Hill and become the largest city in Britain. Not until the 11thC, after many vicissitudes, did London replace Winchester as the capital of England but thereafter its status was secure. By the 19thC the one-time outpost of the Roman Empire had become the hub of the British Empire. That glory has departed but London remains the mother city of the British Commonwealth.

Seldom has a pronouncement, thrown off in a letter, stood the test of time so well as Johnson's observation to Boswell that 'there is in London all that life can afford'. You can extract enjoyment from the metropolis in multiple ways. Just as you can take a temporal approach, by focusing on Georgian London, say, or Victorian London, so you can take a regional one, by focusing on particular districts such as the Docklands, the City of London proper, Soho, Westminster, Greenwich, Chelsea, Notting Hill, Highgate. Or you may wish to concentrate on individual buildings such as St Paul's, the Tower of London, Greenwich Hospital, Westminster Abbey, Buckingham Palace. If you are feeling rich, then you may want to test London's reputation as a mecca for shopping by investigating such venues as Oxford Street, Bond Street, Burlington Arcade, Jermyn Street, Knightsbridge, the King's Road. If your style is more raffish, then you may prefer the ambience of a street market like Portobello Road, Camden Lock, Petticoat Lane or Bermondsey Market. Should the crowds prove a strain, you can find respite walking on Hampstead Heath or strolling in one of London's many parks, Hyde Park for instance, where you can go for a row, practise your golf on the putting green or listen to a concert. Refreshed, you may feel ready to visit a museum perhaps the world-famous British Museum, say, or the Victoria and Albert. And if you are an art-lover don't miss the National Gallery or the Tate or the Whitechapel. In the evening you may want to go to the opera or to a concert, to a performance at Covent Garden perhaps or to a recital at the Queen Elizabeth Hall. But if you prefer the theatre you could take in a comedy on Shaftesbury Avenue or a Shakespearian tradgedy at the Barbican. Finally, if your taste is for ceremony and tradition, then London has plenty to please, try to witness at least one of the following events: Ceremony of the Keys at the Tower of London, Changing the Guard at Buckingham Palace, Trooping the Colour, the State Opening of Parliament, the Lord Mayor's Procession - and Doggett's Coat and Badge Race on the Thames.

And on a fine night you may decide to walk across Hungerford Footbridge with nothing more definite in mind than to look at the view and watch the Thames slip away from you. London provides for every mood.

Elizabeth Claridge

Albert Memorial

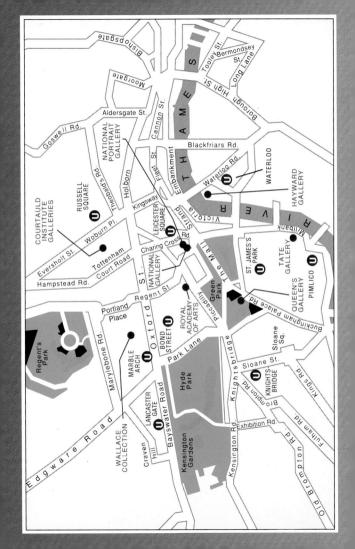

NATIONAL GALLERY Trafalgar Sq., WC2.
• 1000-1800 Mon.-Sat., 1400-1800 Sun. (1000-2000 Wed., June-Aug.).
BR/U Charing Cross. • Free.
Unrivalled display of western European artistic masterpieces.

TATE GALLERY Millbank, SW1.
• 1000-1750 Mon.-Sat., 1400-1750 Sun. U Pimlico. • Free.
British art from the 16thC onwards, and the Clore Gallery devoted to Turner.

ROYAL ACADEMY OF ARTS Burlington House, Piccadilly, W1.
• 1000-1800 Mon.-Sat. U Piccadilly Circus. • Entrance fees vary.
Holds the famous annual summer exhibition of contemporary artists.

WALLACE COLLECTION Hertford House, Manchester Sq, W1.
• 1000-1700 Mon.-Sat., 1400-1700 Sun. U Bond St. • Free.
An impressive collection of 17th and 18thC French art.

COURTAULD INSTITUTE GALLERIES Woburn Sq, WC1.
• 1000-1300, 1400-1700 Mon.-Sat, 1400-1700 Sun.
U Goodge St. • £1.50, child/OAP 50p.
Old Masters as well as French Impressionists and Post-Impressionists.

NATIONAL PORTRAIT GALLERY St Martin's Pl, WC2.
• 1000-1700 Mon.-Sat., 1400-1800 Sun. BR/U Charing Cross. • Free.
A collection of portraits of famous people. Photographs are now included.

QUEEN'S GALLERY Buckingham Palace Rd, SW1.
• 1100-1700 Mon.-Sat., 1400-1700 Sun. U Victoria. • £1.20, child 60p.
Paintings and art treasures from the royal collections.

HAYWARD GALLERY South Bank Centre, SE1.
• 1000-2000 Mon.-Wed. (1800 Thurs.-Sat.), 1200-1800 Sun.
BR/U Waterloo. • Entrance fees vary
Temporary exhibitions of British, American and European artists.

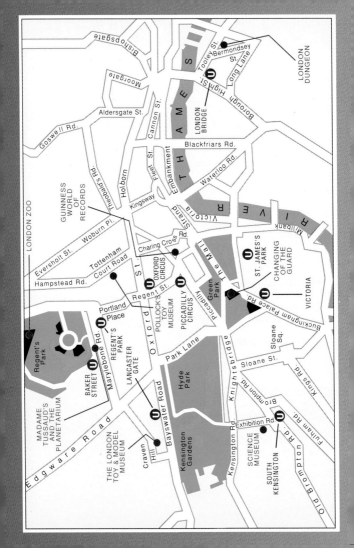

LONDON ZOO Regent's Park, NW1.
• 0900-1800 (summer), 1000-1600 (winter). U Regent's Park.
• £4.30, child under 15 £2.60, under 5s free.
Full of exotic mammals, birds and reptiles. The Children's Zoo contains a variety of friendly animals.

SCIENCE MUSEUM Exhibition Rd, SW7.
• 1000-1800 Mon.-Sat., 1100-1800 Sun. U South Kensington.
• £2.00, child £1.00.
Have fun with science and technology in the activity area.

CHANGING OF THE GUARD Buckingham Palace, SW1.
• 1130 daily Apr.-mid-Aug., alternate days in winter. U St James's Park.
A colourful spectacle of military pomp and pageantry.

GUINNESS WORLD OF RECORDS Piccadilly Circus, W1.
• 1000-2200. U Piccadilly Circus. • £3.80, child £2.40.
The world of superlatives, with life-size exhibits, models and videos.

POLLOCK'S TOY MUSEUM 1 Scala St., W1.
• 1000-1700 Mon.-Sat. U Goodge St.• 80p, child 40p.
Delightful collection of antique toys, dolls and games.

MADAME TUSSAUD'S Marylebone Rd, NW1.
• 1000-1730. U Baker St. • £4.30, child under 15 £2.80.
See your favourite pop star or shiver with fright in the chamber of horrors .

LONDON DUNGEON 28-34 Tooley St., SE1.
• 1000-1730. U London Bridge.• £4.50, child £2.50.
Methods of torture and execution used in Medieval England vividly depicted. Wonderfully gruesome, and only suitable for older children.

THE LONDON TOY AND MODEL MUSEUM Craven Hill, W2.
• 1000-1730 Tues.-Sat., 1100-1730 Sun. U Queensway.
• £2.20, child £1.10.
Toys from through the ages and steam travel on a miniature railway.

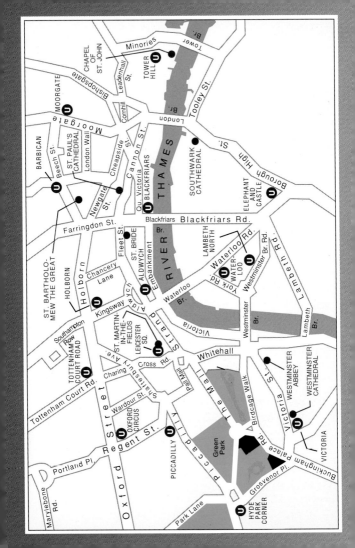

CHURCHES

ST PAUL'S CATHEDRAL Ludgate Hill, EC4.
U St Paul's. •Admission charge for certain sections.
Wren's greatest work is an architectural masterpiece, from the great painted dome to the memorials in the crypt. See **A-Z.**

WESTMINSTER ABBEY Broad Sanctuary, SW1.
•0900-1600 Mon.-Fri. 0900-1400, 1545-1700 Sat. U Westminster.
•Entry to Royal Chapels: £2.00, child £1.00 (free 1800-1945 Wed.).
Superb Gothic structure. The site of royal coronations since 1066. See **A-Z.**

WESTMINSTER CATHEDRAL Ashley Pl, SW1.
•0645-2000. BR/U Victoria.
Roman Catholic cathedral built in 1903 in the Byzantine style, with an ornate marble and mosaic interior.

ST BARTHOLOMEW THE GREAT West Smithfield, EC1.
•0800-1600 (1045 Fri.), 0800-2000 Sun. U St Paul's.
London's oldest parish church, founded in 1123 and restored in the 1860s.

ST BRIDE Fleet St., EC4.
•Museum 0900-1700. U Blackfriars.
Wren's famous 'wedding cake' steeple. The museum in the crypt reflects the history of Fleet St. and the church's role as the 'printers' church.

SOUTHWARK CATHEDRAL Borough High St., SE1.
U London Bridge.
One of London's most impressive medieval buildings.

CHAPEL OF ST JOHN Tower of London, EC3.
•0930-1700 Mon.-Sat., 1400-1700 Sun. U Tower Hill.
•£4.50, child £2.00.
One of the finest examples of Norman architecture in England.

ST MARTIN-IN-THE-FIELDS Trafalgar Sq, WC2.
Lunchtime concerts. BR/U Charing Cross.
This Grecian-style building is the Queen's parish church.

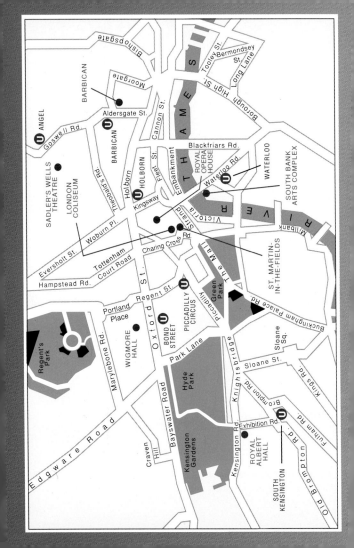

SOUTH BANK ARTS COMPLEX South Bank, SE1.
BR/U Waterloo.
Visit Festival Hall to hear the British Symphony Orchestra, Queen Elizabeth Hall for chamber music and the Purcell Room for solo recitals.

ROYAL ALBERT HALL Kensington Gore, SW7.
U South Kensington.
Superb Victorian concert hall which is best known as the home of the Sir Henry Wood Promenade Concerts (the Proms) from July to September.

BARBICAN HALL Barbican Centre, EC2.
U Barbican (closed Sun.), Moorgate.
Home of the London Symphony Orchestra who regularly perform here.

ROYAL OPERA HOUSE Bow St., WC2.
Box office in Floral St. U Covent Garden.
Home of the world-famous Royal Ballet and Royal Opera Companies.

LONDON COLISEUM St Martin's Lane, WC2.
U Charing Cross.
One of the largest auditoria in London. The Coliseum is home to the English National Opera.

WIGMORE HALL Wigmore St., W1.
U Oxford Circus, Bond St.
This famous concert hall features young, lesser-known soloists.

SADLER'S WELLS THEATRE Rosebery Av, EC1.
U Angel Islington.
Home of the Sadler's Wells Ballet Company as well as venue for operettas (including Gilbert & Sullivan).

ST MARTIN-IN-THE-FIELDS Trafalgar Sq, WC2.
U Charing Cross.
Lunchtime concerts of chamber and choral music are held daily in the pleasing setting of this famous church.

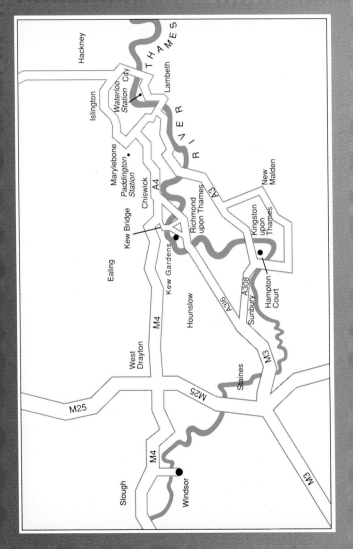

EXCURSIONS

West

One day

Kew Gardens - 11 km west of central London. U Kew Gardens/BR Waterloo to Kew Bridge. The Royal Botanic Gardens: 1000-till dusk. Greenhouses, museum and galleries: 1100-1730 (dusk in winter). Plant varieties from all over the world are grown and studied at this scientific institution. The grounds also contain the superb Palm House, a greenhouse for tropical plants (built in 1844), and the 17thC Kew Palace, the summer home of King George III. There is also the Orangery (1861) which houses temporary exhibitions as well as a library. See **PARKS.**

Hampton Court, Hampton, Middlesex - 24 km south west of central London. BR Waterloo to Hampton Court. 0930-1800 Mon.-Sat., 1100-1800 Sun. (summer); 0930-1700 Mon.-Fri., 1400-1700 Sun. (winter). Built in the early 1500 s for Henry VIII's court favourite, Cardinal Wolsey. The apotheosis of Tudor style, the palace was later modified in the early 1700s by Wren. A tour round the impressive buildings should include the Clock Court, State Apartments, Great Hall and the lovely Fountain Court. The grounds contain the famous Hampton Court Maze.

Windsor - 34 km west of London. BR Paddington to Windsor Riverside or Waterloo to Windsor Central. The castle is the royal family's main residence outside London. It is the oldest and largest inhabited castle in the world. The State Apartments and Queen Mary's Doll's House are open to the public. Climb the Round Tower to enjoy the splendid views from the top; visit the State Apartments, with their collection of drawings by Michelangelo, Rembrandt and de Vinci; and admire the beautiful Gothic Chapel of St George. The Savill Gardens can also be visited (1000-1800 Mar.-Nov.) as well as Windsor Great Park whose wooded grounds extend to Ascot racetrack. See also Madame Tussaud's waxworks at Windsor Station. On the other side of the river is Eton and its famous college. Founded in 1450 by King Henry VI, this public school is to open to visitors (1400-1700 Mon.-Fri.,1000-1700 during public holidays).

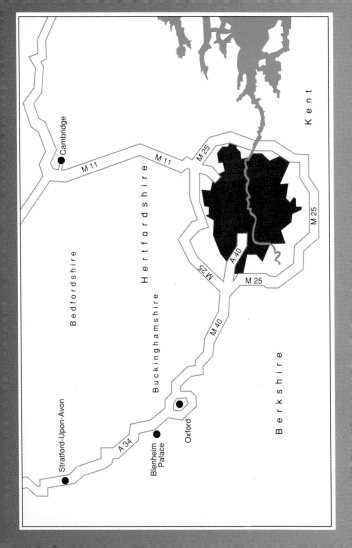

North

One day

Oxford - 90 km north west of London. BR Paddington to Oxford (approx. 90 min). By car: A 40 and M 40 (approx. 90 min). Car drivers are advised to park on the outskirts of the city as the centre is mainly pedestrianized.

This ancient university town possesses a unique atmosphere, combining respect for tradition and learning, enshrined in its rich architectural heritage, with the youthful high spirits of student life. The Ashmolean Museum in Beaumont St. (1100-1600 Mon.-Sat., 1400-1600 Sun.) is one of the most beautiful in Britain and contains archaeological relics, medieval art treasures, a rich collection of silverware and drawings by Michelangelo and Raphael. Visit High St. and Broad St., lined with superb buildings, New College (which is in fact one of the oldest, dating from 1379) and Magdalene College, undoubtedly the most beautiful in Oxford, with its Gothic tower. Contact the local tourist board for details of guided tours around the university buildings and the magnificent Bodleian Library.

Stratford-upon-Avon - 155 km north west of London, 65 km north of Oxford. BR Paddington and connection at Leamington Spa (approx. 2 hr 30 min) or Euston to Coventry, then local bus (approx. 2 hr). By car: A 40 and M 40 to Oxford, then A 34. Most travel agencies can arrange bookings for organized coach tours from London. Shakespeare's birthplace is a must for all tourists to visit. His house (0900-1800 Mon.-Sat., 1330-1630 Sun.) contains the room where he was born in April 1564 . He died at New Place aged 52, and is buried in the cemetery in Trinity Street. The Royal Shakespeare Company puts on up to six plays at the Royal Shakespeare Theatre in Waterside during the autumn season, a wonderful opportunity for theatre-lovers to experience Shakespearian drama performed by the world's top actors. For further information and reservations tel: (0789) 69191. Also worth visiting are the Bancroft Gardens. Three kilometres west of Stratford (bus from American fountain) is the cottage where Anne Hathaway, Shakespeare's second wife, was born and lived up until the time of her marriage to the Bard of Avon . His mother, Mary Arden's house is at Wilmcote some six kilometres outside Stratford. It now contains an agricultural museum.

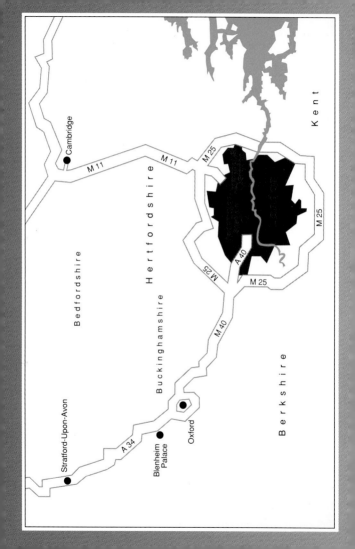

Cambridge - 86 km north east of London. BR Liverpool St. to Cambridge (approx. 75 min). By car: M 11 (approx. 90 min). Tourist Office: Wheeler St., tel: (0223) 322640.

This town is world famous for its colleges, which exhibit a wealth of architectural features. Many of them are open to the public, and among the most notable are Peterhouse, the oldest, which dates from 1281; Emmanuel and Pembroke with their College Chapels, both of which were designed by Wren; and the superb Gothic perpendicular chapel of King's College which contains Ruben's *Adoration of the Magi.* Be sure to see Trinity College, the largest in Cambridge, and Queen's College, with its bridge over the River Cam. Also visit the Fitzwilliam Museum in Trumpington St. (1000-1700 Tues.-Sat., 1415-1700 Sun.) which contains an impressive art collection, including works by Gainsborough, Turner, Rembrandt and Renoir.

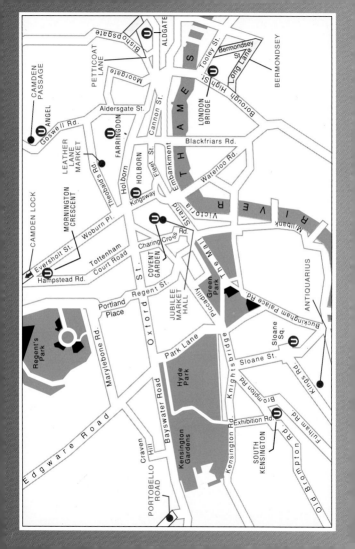

PORTOBELLO ROAD, Portobello Rd, W11.
- 0800-1600 Mon., Tues., Wed., Fri., 0800-1300 Thurs., 0800-1800 Sat.
U Notting Hill Gate, Ladbroke Grove.
Famous flea market good for antiques, memorabilia, clothes and food.

CAMDEN PASSAGE Camden Passage, N1.
- 0645-1600 Wed., 0700-1600 Thurs., 0800-1700 Sat. U Angel.
Over 350 antique dealers have stalls here on Wednesdays and Saturdays. Books, prints and drawings are sold on Thursdays.

CAMDEN LOCK Camden High St., NW1.
- 0900-1800 Sat., Sun. U Camden Town.
Fashionable weekend market for crafts, bric-a-brac, health foods and jewellery. Main market is adjacent to Regent's Canal.

PETTICOAT LANE Petticoat Lane, E1.
- 0900-1400 Sun. U Liverpool St., Aldgate East.
Typical East End Sunday market. Tends to become very crowded after 1100.

BERMONDSEY Long Lane and Bermondsey St., SE1.
- 0500-1400 Fri. BR/U London Bridge.
Covered market selling glass, silver and brassware, maps and prints.

JUBILEE MARKET HALL Covent Garden, WC2.
- 0900-1700 Tues.-Sun., 0600-1700 Mon. U Covent Garden.
Mondays for antiques, Tuesdays to Fridays for crafts, clothes and foods and weekends for handicrafts.

LEATHER LANE MARKET Leather Lane, EC1.
- 1000-1430 Mon.-Fri. U Chancery Lane.
Typical street market selling household goods, clothes, plants, fruit and veg.

ANTIQUARIUS 135 King's Rd, SW3.
- 1000-1800 Mon.-Sat. U Sloane Sq.
This covered antique market has over 170 dealers selling antiques and unusual fashions.

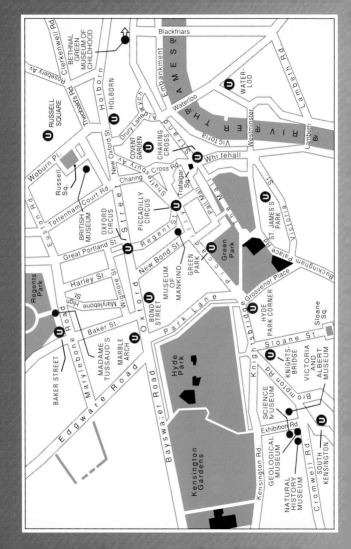

BRITISH MUSEUM Great Russell St., WC1.
•1000-1700 Mon.-Sat., 1430-1800 Sun. U Russell Sq, Tottenham
Court Rd. •Free (except for special exhibitions).
Superb collection covering a wide range of cultures and subjects. See **A-Z**.

VICTORIA AND ALBERT MUSEUM Cromwell Rd, SW7.
•1000-1750 Mon.-Sat., 1430-1750 Sun. U South Kensington.
•£2.00, child 50p.
Possibly the world's greatest collection of applied art and design. **See A-Z.**

SCIENCE MUSEUM Exhibition Rd, SW7.
•1000-1800 Mon.-Sat. (1100 Sun.). U South Kensington.
•£2.00, child £1.00.
Excellent coverage of scientific discoveries and applications. See **A-Z**.

NATURAL HISTORY MUSEUM & GEOLOGICAL MUSEUM
Cromwell Rd, SW7.
•1000-1800 Mon.-Sat., 1300-1800 Sun. U South Kensington.
•£2.50, child £1.25 (free 1630-1800 Mon.-Fri., 1700-1800 Sat., Sun.).
A unique opportunity to experience the wonders of natural history.

MUSEUM OF MANKIND Burlington Gardens, W1.
•1000-1700 Mon.-Sat. 1400-1800 Sun. U Piccadilly Circus. •Free.
Sculptures, pottery, masks and other artefacts from different cultures.

MADAME TUSSAUD'S/PLANETARIUM Marylebone Rd, NW1.
•1000-1730 Mon.-Fri., 0930-1730 Sat., Sun. U Baker St.
•Combined ticket £6.10, child £3.80.
*Enjoy the Chamber of Horrors, historical tableaux and famous personalities
of the wax museum, and the Planetarium's breath-taking depiction of space.*

BETHNAL GREEN MUSEUM OF CHILDHOOD
Cambridge Heath Rd, Bethnal Green, E2.
•1000-1750 Mon.-Thurs. & Sat., 1430-1750 Sun.
U Bethnal Green.•Free.
Massive collection of children's toys, games, books and clothes.

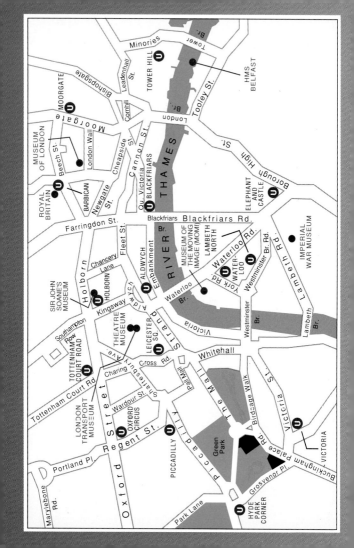

MUSEUM OF LONDON London Wall, EC2.
•1000-1800 Tues.-Sat., 1400-1800 Sun. ∪ St. Paul's. •Free.
The daily life of the city through the ages. Historical street scenes. See **A-Z**.

ROYAL BRITAIN Barbican Centre, Aldersgate St., EC2.
•0900-1730. ∪ Barbican (closed Sun.). •£3.95, child £2.50.
A lively exhibition surveying 1000 years of British royal history.

LONDON TRANSPORT MUSEUM Covent Garden, WC2.
•1000-1800. ∪ Covent Garden. •£2.40, child £1.10.
Trains, trams and buses from past to present. See **WALK 2**.

THEATRE MUSEUM Covent Garden, WC2.
•1100-1900. ∪ Covent Garden. •£2.25, child £1.25.
The national museum of the performing arts. See **WALK 2**.

MUSEUM OF THE MOVING IMAGE (MOMI)
South Bank Arts Complex, Waterloo, SE1.
•1000-2000 Tues.-Sat., 1000-1800 Sun. ∪ Waterloo.
•£3.25, child £2.50.
Impressive exhibits illustrating the history of television and the cinema.

SIR JOHN SOANE'S MUSEUM 13 Lincoln's Inn Fields, WC2.
•1000-1700 Tues.-Sat. ∪ Holborn.
The eccentric art and antiquities collection of 19thC architect John Soane.

IMPERIAL WAR MUSEUM Lambeth Rd, SE1.
•1000-1750 Mon.-Sat., 1400-1750 Sun.
∪ Lambeth North, Elephant & Castle. •£2.50, child £1.25.
Exhibits cover all aspects of 20thC warfare, and are housed in the once notorious Bedlam Hospital for the insane.

HMS BELFAST Morgans Lane, Tooley St., SE1.
•0900-1700. ∪ London Bridge (access via Hays Galleria, or by motor launch from pier by Tower of London). •£3.60, child £1.90.
One of the largest Royal Navy cruisers ever built . Now a floating museum.

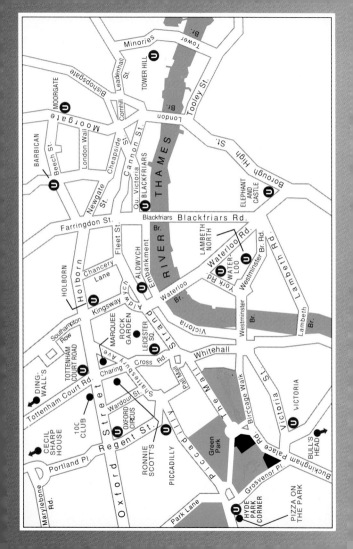

100 CLUB 100 Oxford St., W1.
• 1930-2400 Mon.-Thurs., 1930-0100 Fri.-Sat., 1930-2330 Sun.
U Tottenham Court Rd. • £2.50-£6.00 depending on artist.
Jazz club featuring all the big names and sounds in jazz.

RONNIE SCOTT'S 47 Frith St., W1.
• 2030-0300. U Leicester Sq • £8.00-£10.00 depending on artist.
The premier venue for all jazz lovers. Reservations recommended.

PIZZA ON THE PARK 11 Knightsbridge, SW1.
U Hyde Park Corner.
This pizza restaurant has excellent jazz bands playing nightly (except Sun.).

BULL'S HEAD Barnes, SW13.
BR Barnes Bridge (from Waterloo Station).
*This pub beside the Thames on the outskirts of the city, is a jazz connois-
seur's delight. Excellent bands every night.*

CECIL SHARP HOUSE 2 Regent's Park Rd, NW1.
U Camden Town.
*Club specializing in folk acts. Reservations are advisable for the more popu-
lar artists.*

ROCK GARDEN 6-7 The Piazza, Covent Garden, WC2.
U Covent Garden.
*Regular rock venue in the city centre with a lively bar and diner serving
burgers and chilli.*

MARQUEE 105 Charing Cross Rd, WC2.
U Leicester Sq.
*Some of the world's greatest bands first made a name for themselves at this
popular venue.*

DINGWALLS Camden Lock, Chalk Farm, NW1.
U Camden Town.
Contemporary rock and jazz venue. Live music every night.

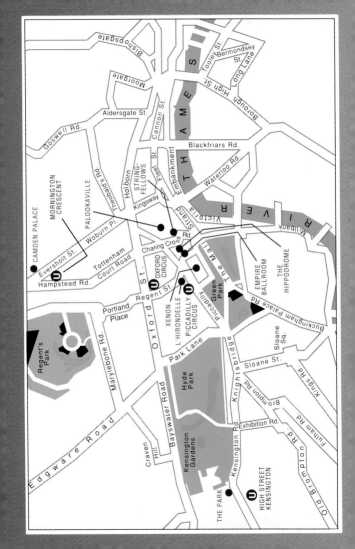

STRINGFELLOWS 16-19 St Martin's Lane, WC2.
• 2000-0330. ᑌ Leicester Sq. • £6.00-£12.00.
Fashionable venue frequented by the rich and famous pursued by the paparazzi. Strict entrance policy.

THE PARK 38 Kensington High St., W8.
• 1000-0300 Mon.-Sat., private parties only Tues.,Fri. ᑌ High St. Kensington.
• £3.00-£7.00.
Trendy crowd in this fashionable disco with smart bar and restaurant.

THE HIPPODROME Charing Cross Rd and Cranbourne St., WC2.
• 2100-0330 Mon.-Sat. ᑌ Leicester Sq. • £6.00-£10.00.
Popular venue with massive sound system, lasers, videos, closed-circuit TV.

CAMDEN PALACE Camden High St., NW1.
• 2100-0300 Tues.-Sat. ᑌ Mornington Cresc, Camden. • £4.00-£5.00.
Sophisticated disco with elaborate lights and sounds, bar and restaurant.

EMPIRE BALLROOM Leicester Sq, WC2.
• 2200-0200 Mon.-Sat., 2200-0100 Sun. ᑌ Leicester Sq • £3.50-£5.00.
Informal atmosphere with good lighting and sound system.

XENON 196 Piccadilly, W1.
• 2100-0300 Mon.-Sat. ᑌ Piccadilly Circus. • £5.00-£8.00.
Attracts a cosmopolitan crowd. Disco music, cabaret, dancers.

L'HIRONDELLE Swallow St., W1.
• 2030-0330. ᑌ Piccadilly Circus. • £7.50 for non-diners.
Restaurant with international menu, dancing and a flamboyant cabaret.

PALOOKAVILLE 13a St James St., WC1.
• 2100-0015 (wine bar open to 0115) Mon.-Fri.
ᑌ Covent Garden. • Admission free.
Basement restaurant and wine bar decorated in New York club style, with jazz musicians playing to a lively young audience.

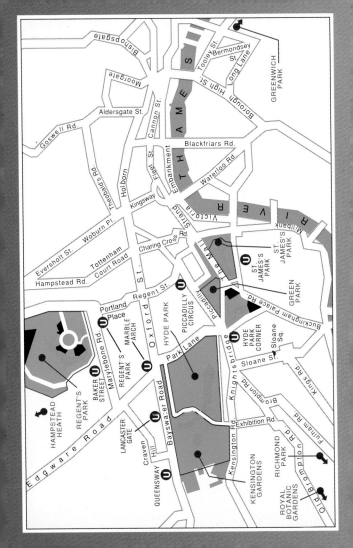

HYDE PARK Hyde Park, W2.
U Hyde Park Corner, Marble Arch, Queensway, Lancaster Gate.
*Large central park offering a wide range of activities. See **A-Z**.*

KENSINGTON GARDENS Kensington Gardens, SW2.
U Lancaster Gate, Queensway.
Surrounding the London residence of the Prince of Wales.

GREEN PARK Green Park, W1.
U Green Park.
*Smallest of the royal parks near Buckingham Palace (see **SIGHTSEEING**, **A-Z**).*

ST JAMES'S PARK Saint James's Park, SW2.
U St James's Park.
Enjoy a walk through the gardens, feed the ducks or listen to a concert.

REGENT'S PARK Regent's Park, NW1.
U Regent's Park, Camden Town. Bus 74.
*Enjoy Queen Mary's Gardens or drama in the open-air theatre. See **A-Z**.*

GREENWICH PARK Greenwich, SE10.
BR Greenwich, Maze Hill. Boats from Westminster, Charing Cross.
*Rises steeply from the river to give a panoramic city view. See **WALK 4**.*

RICHMOND PARK Richmond, Surrey.
BR/U Richmond, then bus no. 65 or 71.
*Herds of red and fallow deer roam freely in scenic woodland. See **A-Z**.*

HAMPSTEAD HEATH Hampstead Heath, NW3.
U Hampstead. BR Gospel Oak, Hampstead Heath.
*Wild, open heath and woodland. Impressive views of London. See **A-Z**.*

ROYAL BOTANIC GARDENS Kew, Richmond, Surrey.
•1000-2000 Summer, 1000-1600 Winter.
BR/U Kew Gardens. •£1.00, child 50p.
*One of the greatest plant collections in Europe. See **EXCURSION 1**.*

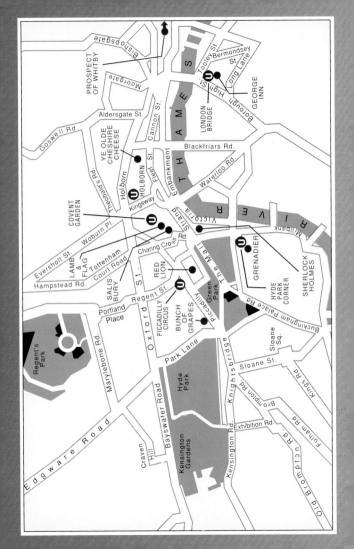

YE OLDE CHESHIRE CHEESE Wine Office Court, EC4.
U Temple.
This pub, just north of Fleet St., was Dr Johnson's favourite hostelry.

PROSPECT OF WHITBY 57 Wapping Wall, E1.
U Wapping.
Famous East End riverside pub built in 1520, with a history of associations with pirates and smugglers.

SHERLOCK HOLMES 10 Northumberland St., WC2.
U Charing Cross.
Inside is an interesting small 'museum' devoted to the great detective.

LAMB AND FLAG Rose St., WC2.
U Covent Garden.
*The oldest pub in Covent Garden (see **WALK 2**), and always crowded.*

RED LION 2 Duke of York St., SW1.
U Piccadilly Circus.
Superb Victorian gin palace with mahogany panelling and cut glass decor.

GRENADIER 18 Wilton Row, SW1.
U Hyde Park Corner.
Charming pub located in a mews. Excellent bar food.

SALISBURY Cecil Court, St Martin's Lane, W1.
U Charing Cross.
Beautiful Art Nouveau decor and a cosmopolitan atmosphere.

GEORGE INN 77 Borough High St., SE1.
U London Bridge.
London's last surviving galleried coaching-inn. Shakespeare performed here.

BUNCH OF GRAPES 16 Shepherd Market, W1.
U Green Park.
Traditional Victorian pub in the heart of Mayfair.

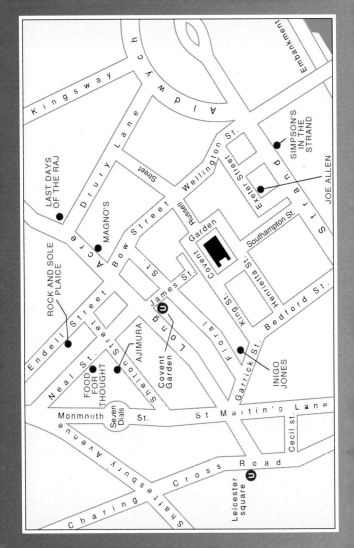

INIGO JONES 14 Garrick St., WC2.
- Closed Sat. lunchtime and all day Sun. U Covent Garden.
- Expensive.

French nouvelle cuisine served in a beautiful setting.

MAGNO'S 65a Long Acre, WC2.
- Closed Sat. pm, Sun. all day. U Covent Garden. • Moderate-Expensive.

Traditional-style French brasserie with excellent pre-opera menu.

SIMPSON'S IN THE STRAND 100 Strand, WC2.
- Closed Sun. U Covent Garden. • Medium-Expensive.

For the real taste of Old England: roast beef, Aylesbury duck and apple pie.

LAST DAYS OF THE RAJ 22 Drury Lane, WC2.
- 1200-1430 & 1730-2330 Mon.-Sat., 1800-2300 Sun.
U Covent Garden, Aldwych. • Medium.

Impeccable Indian food served in a light and spacious setting.

JOE ALLEN 13 Exeter St., WC2.
- 1200-0045 Mon.-Sat., 1200-1145 Sun. U Covent Garden. • Medium.

Good spot to enjoy great burgers, BBQ ribs, huge bowls of salad and luscious brownies.

AJIMURA 51-53 Shelton St., WC2.
- 1200-1500 & 1800-2300 Mon.-Fri., 1800-2300 Sat., 1800-2230 Sun.
U Covent Garden. • Medium.

Japanese cuisine. Specialities for the initiated and good-value set meals.

FOOD FOR THOUGHT 31 Neal St., WC2.
- 1200-2000 Mon.-Fri. U Covent Garden. • Budget.

Popular vegetarian restaurant. Delicious salads, soups and pasta dishes.

ROCK AND SOLE PLAICE 47 Endell St., WC2.
- 1130-2200 Mon.-Sat. U Covent Garden. • Budget.

This is the spot to try good old-fashioned fish and chips. Cod and plaice are traditional, but more imaginative fish dishes are also available.

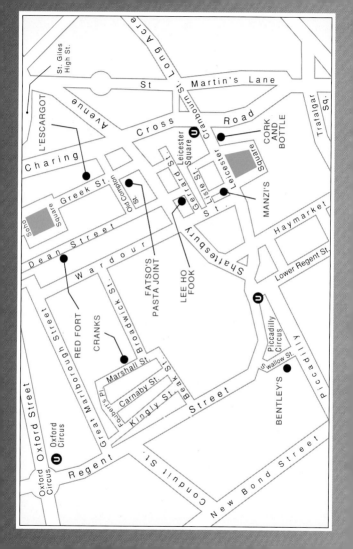

L'ESCARGOT 48 Greek St., W1.
• 1200-1500, 1730-2315 Mon.-Fri., 1800-2355 Sat.
U Tottenham Court Rd, Leicester Sq. •Expensive.
Refined French cuisine which has been adapted to London tastes and expectations. Choose from the brasserie or the main restaurant.

CORK AND BOTTLE 44-46 Cranbourn St., WC2.
• 1100-1500, 1730-2300 Mon.-Sat., 1200-1400/1900-2230 Sun.
U Leicester Sq. •Budget.
Wine bar offering a variety of delicous buffet meals. Impressive wine list.

FATSO'S PASTA JOINT 13 Old Compton St., W1.
• 1200-2400 Mon.-Thurs., 1200-0100 Fri.-Sat., 1200-2300 Sun.
U Tottenham Ct Rd, Leicester Sq. •Budget.
Wonderful selection of pasta dishes with delicious sauces.

BENTLEY'S 11 Swallow St., W1.
• 1200-1500 & 1800-2300 Mon.-Sat. U Piccadilly Circus. •Expensive.
One of the best seafood restaurants in London.

MANZI'S 1 Leicester St., WC2.
• 1200-1430 & 1730-2315 Mon.-Sat., 1800-2200 Sun.
U Leicester Sq. •Medium.
Italian cuisine including wonderful seafood dishes. Excellent value.

RED FORT 77 Dean St., W1.
• Till 2315 Mon.-Sat., till 2245 Sun. U Leicester Sq. •Medium.
Modern Indian cuisine, mostly dishes from northern India.

LEE HO FOOK 15-16 Gerrard St., W1.
• 1200-2330 Mon.-Sat. 1200-2230 Sun. U Leicester Sq. •Medium.
Right in the heart of Chinatown. Excellent Dim Sum.

CRANKS 8 Marshall St., W1.
• 0800-2230 Mon.-Fri., 0900-2230 Sat. U Oxford Circus. •Budget.
London's most famous vegetarian restaurant, with a wide-ranging menu.

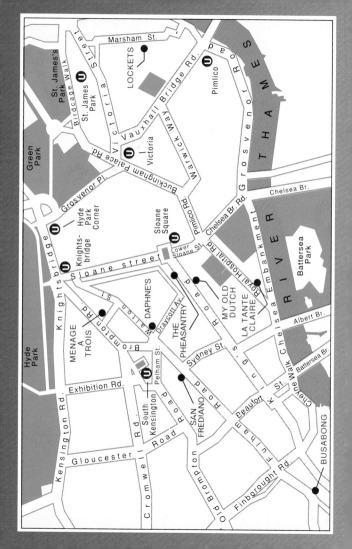

LA TANTE CLAIRE 68 Royal Hospital Rd, SW3.
•1230-1400, 1900-2300 Mon.-Fri Closed Sat., Sun., Easter and August.
U Sloane Sq. •Expensive.
Renowned for its French haute cuisine. Two Michelin stars.

DAPHNE'S 12 Draycott Ave, SW3.
•1230-1430 & 1930-2345 Mon.-Fri., 1930-2345 Sat.
U South Kensington. •Medium-Expensive.
Classical and inventive French dishes. Smart, but unpretentious.

LOCKETS Marsham Court, Marsham St., SW1.
•1215-1430, 1830-2300 Mon.-Fri., 1830-2300 Sat.
U Westminster, Pimlico. •Medium.
Superb traditional English dishes. Popular with neighbouring MPs.

MY OLD DUTCH 267 Kings Rd, SW3.
•Daily till 2330. U Sloane Sq. •Budget.
Sweet and savoury pancakes. Pleasant delft-blue decor.

MENAGE À TROIS 15 Beauchamp Pl, SW3.
•1130-1445 & 1900-0015 Mon.-Fri., 1900-0015 Sat., 1900-2300 Sun.
U Knightsbridge. •Medium.
Perfect spot for a health food meal or snack after Harrods (see **SHOPPING***).*

THE PHEASANTRY 152 Kings Rd, SW3.
•1830-0200. U Sloane Sq. •Budget-Medium.
Restored building containing two Italian restaurants, cocktail bar, and disco.

SAN FREDIANO 62 Fulham Rd, SW3.
•1230-1430, 1915-2315 Mon.-Sat. U South Kensington. •Medium.
Exquisite Tuscan cuisine and an excellent selection of wines.

BUSABONG 331 Fulham Rd, SW3.
•1800-2315 Mon., 1230-2315 Tues.-Sat., 1230-2230 Sun.
U South Kensington. •Budget-Medium.
Thai food served in a variety of settings in a complex covering three floors.

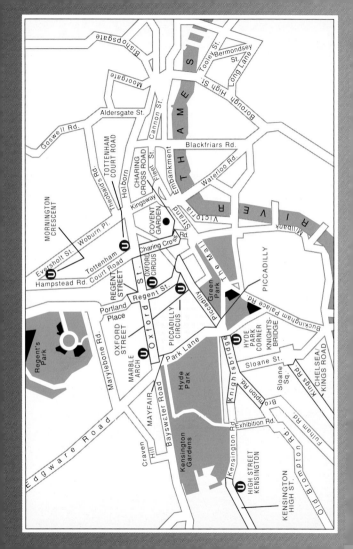

SHOPPING AREAS

OXFORD STREET U Oxford Circus, Bond Street, Marble Arch.
Britain's busiest shopping street features Selfridges and several major department stores. See SHOPPING, **Shopping and Best Buys**.

COVENT GARDEN U Covent Garden.
Dominated by the shopping piazza in the former fruit and vegetable market. Quality boutiques and speciality shops predominate. See WALK 2.

KNIGHTSBRIDGE U Knightsbridge.
Knightsbridge is synonymous with Harrods which sets the standard for shops in this area. Investigate the unusual boutiques around Beauchamp Pl.

KENSINGTON HIGH STREET U High Street Kensington.
Not as hectic or congested as the West End, but has a similar range of chain and fashion stores.

CHELSEA/KINGS ROAD U Sloane Square.
Definitely the area to come to for the latest fashions as well as an outing to the King's Road on a Saturday afternoon. See **A-Z.**

PICCADILLY U Piccadilly, Green Park.
The elegant Jermyn Street and St James's Street make Piccadilly synonymous with high-class gentlemen's shopping.

CHARING CROSS ROAD U Tottenham Court Rd, Leicester Sq.
Book shops galore - Foyle's is the world's largest. The area also has many excellent music shops.

REGENT STREET U Piccadilly Circus, Oxford Circus.
The up-market ambience of the grand street is typified in Liberty's and Garrards, the crown jewellers.

MAYFAIR U Bond Street.
Old and New Bond Street, Savile Row and Burlington Arcade emphasize traditional and expensive British goods.

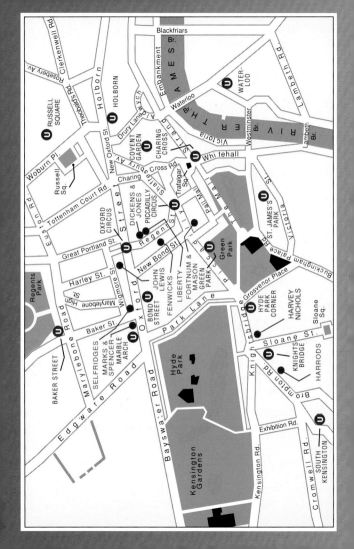

HARRODS Brompton Rd, SW1.
• 0900-1800 Mon., Tues., Thurs.-Sat.,0930-1900 Wed. U Knightsbridge.
You can buy just about anything from Harrods. Don't miss the Food Halls.

HARVEY NICHOLS Knightsbridge, W1.
• 1000-1900 Mon.-Fri., 1000-1800 Sat. U Knightsbridge.
High-quality store renowned for its household furnishings and fashions.

LIBERTY Regent St., W1.
. 0930-1800 Mon.-Sat. (1930 Thurs.). U Oxford Circus.
Galleried store specializing in textiles, jewellery, chinaware, oriental rugs.

MARKS & SPENCER 173 and 458 Oxford St., W1.
• 0930 (0900 Sat.)-1800 Mon.-Wed., Sat. (1900 Fri., 2000 Thurs.).
U Oxford Circus.
For woollen items or explore their extensive food department.

SELFRIDGES Oxford St., W1.
• 0930-1800 Mon.-Sat. (2000 Thurs.). U Marble Arch.
Second largest of London's department stores. Good choice of food.

FORTNUM & MASON 181 Piccadilly, W1.
• 0900-1730 Mon.-Sat U Piccadilly Circus.
The aristocrat of grocers. Exotic preserves and other delicacies.

JOHN LEWIS Oxford Circus, W1.
• 0900-1730 Mon.-Wed., Fri., Sat., 0930-2000 Thurs. U Bond St.
Dress fabrics plus a wide selection of linen and kitchenware.

DICKENS & JONES 244 Regent St., W1.
• 0930-1800 Mon.-Wed., Fri., Sat. 0930-2000 Thurs. U Oxford Circus.
Fashions and beauty products. Visit the designer room for the latest styles.

FENWICKS 63 New Bond St., W1.
• 0930-1800 Mon.-Wed., Fri., Sat. 0930-1930 Thurs. U Bond St.
Quality goods ranging from clothing to cookware.

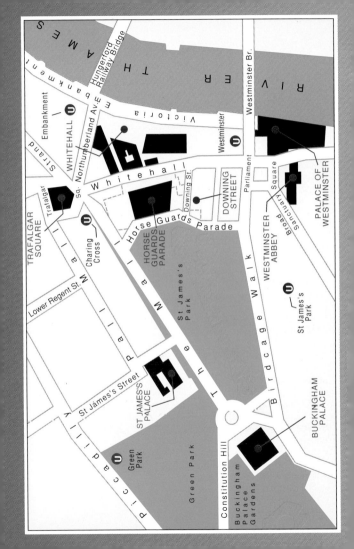

BUCKINGHAM PALACE
Closed except for Queen's Gallery (see **ART GALLERIES**) and Royal Mews.
U Victoria, Hyde Park Corner.
*Official residence of the monarch since Queen Victoria. When the royal
standard is flying, the Queen is in residence. See* **A-Z.**

PALACE OF WESTMINSTER Parliament Sq, SW1.
U Westminster.
*Home of the 'mother of parliaments'. Access to the buildings is restricted for
security reasons. See* **A-Z**.

ST JAMES'S PALACE Pall Mall, SW1.
U Green Park.
*Formerly the favourite royal palace, St James's now houses royal offices and
Clarence House, the home of H. M. The Queen Mother.*

WHITEHALL
U Charing Cross, Westminster.
Government ministries, the centre of British government. See **WALK 1.**

HORSE GUARDS PARADE Whitehall, SW1.
U Charing Cross, Westminster.
See the household cavalry on sentry duty in Whitehall. See **WALK 1.**

WESTMINSTER ABBEY Broad Sanctuary, SW1.
U Westminster
*Visit Poets' Corner, the Tomb of the Unknown Warrior and the Coronation
Throne. See* **CHURCHES**, **WALK 1**, **A-Z.**

TRAFALGAR SQUARE Trafalgar Sq, SW1.
U Charing Cross.
Nelson's Column and the fountains. See **A-Z.**

DOWNING STREET 10 Downing St., SW1.
U Westminster, Charing Cross.
Official residence of the Prime Minister since 1735. See **WALK 1.**

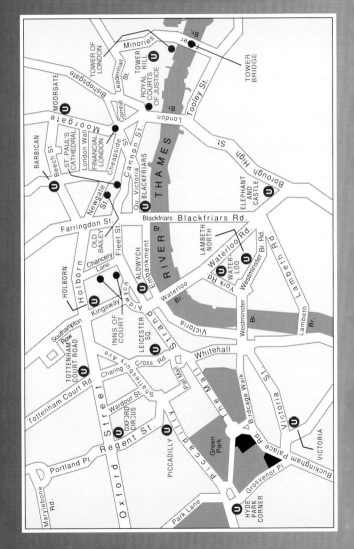

TOWER OF LONDON Tower Hill, EC1.
•0930-1700 Mon.-Sat., 1400-1700 Sun. U Tower Hill.
•£4.50, child £2.00.
It has been a fortress, palace, prison and royal menagerie. Houses the
Crown Jewels and the equally valuable Royal Armouries. See **WALK 3**, **A-Z**.

TOWER BRIDGE
•Museum and Walkways 1000-1830 (1645 Nov.-Mar.).
U Tower Hill. •£2.00, child £1.00.
Built in 1894 and one of the most photographed sights in London. Walk
along the gantries for impressive views of the Thames. See **WALK 3**.

ROYAL COURTS OF JUSTICE Strand, WC2.
•0930-1630 Mon.-Fri. Closed August and September. U Temple.
England's main civil law courts. Trials are open to the public (aged over 14).

OLD BAILEY Old Bailey/Newgate Street.
•1030-1300, 1400-1600 Mon.-Fri. Closed Aug., early Sept. U St Paul's.
The Central Criminal Court. Trials are open to the public (aged over 14).

ST PAUL'S CATHEDRAL Ludgate Hill, EC4.
U St Paul's.
An impressive landmark. Visit the dome and Whispering Gallery. See
CHURCHES, **WALK 3**, **A-Z**.

FINANCIAL LONDON Bank, EC2.
U Bank.
The Bank of England, Stock Exchange, Royal Exchange and Mansion House
(official residence of the Lord Mayor of London). See **WALK 3**.

INNS OF COURT
Gray's Inn WC1, Lincoln's Inn WC2,
Middle Temple and Inner Temple EC4.
U Chancery Lane, Holborn, Temple.
The historic training-grounds of English barristers. Public access is available
to some buildings.

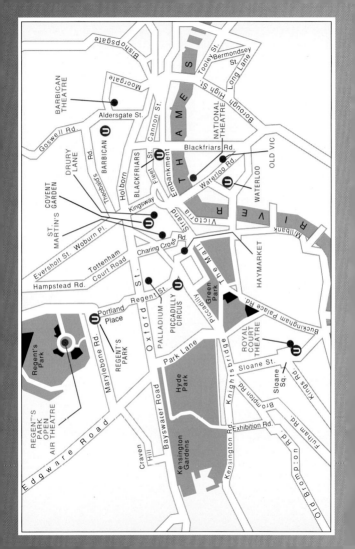

NATIONAL THEATRE South Bank Arts Complex, SE1.
BR/U Waterloo.
A wide range of the highest quality international and British productions are staged in the Lyttelton, Olivier and Cottesloe theatres.

ROYAL COURT THEATRE Sloane Sq, SW1.
U *Sloane Square.*
Oldest of the avant-garde theatres. Premiered works by Shaw and Osborne.

BARBICAN THEATRE Barbican Theatre, EC2.
U Barbican (Moorgate on Sun.).
London home of the Royal Shakespeare Company. See **A-Z.**

HAYMARKET Theatre Royal, Haymarket, SW1.
U Piccadilly Circus.
This elegant theatre stages classical and modern plays.

PALLADIUM Argyll St., W1.
U Oxford Circus.
London theatre famous for variety shows, musicals and pantomimes.

DRURY LANE Theatre Royal, Catherine St., WC2.
U Covent Garden.
The oldest surviving theatre in London. Musicals are its speciality.

OLD VIC Waterloo Rd, SE1.
U Waterloo.
Lovely early 19thC theatre producing British and European classics.

ST MARTIN'S West St., Cambridge Circus.
U Leicester Sq.
For Agatha Christie lovers. The Mousetrap has played here since 1952.

REGENT'S PARK OPEN AIR THEATRE
Queen Mary's Gardens, Regent's Park, NW1. U Regent's Park.
The summer season of Shakespearian drama is not to be missed. See **PARKS.**

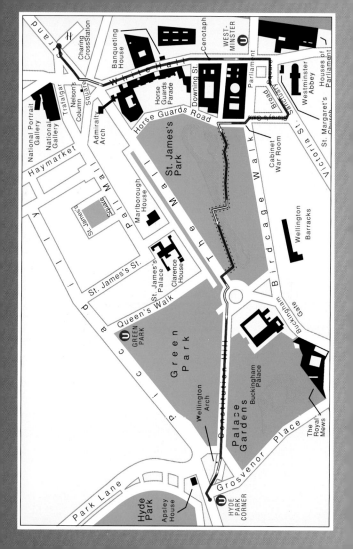

Westminster

Begin at Charing Cross Station.

In the forecourt is a replica of the original Charing Cross (1290) which marked the last stop of the funeral cortege of Eleanor, wife of Edward I. Turn left down the Strand across Northumberland Av, then left again to the top of Whitehall. From here one can look across Trafalgar Square with its fountains, stone lions and pigeons (see **A-Z**). Dominating the north side of the square is the National Gallery building (see **ART GALLERIES**). Proceed down Whitehall to Banqueting House (1000-1700 Tues.-Sat., 1400-1700 Sun. 80p, child 40p) which was designed by Inigo Jones (1622) for James I as part of the Palace of Whitehall. The magnificent ceiling, painted by Rubens, was commissioned by Charles I in 1629. Cross Whitehall to the entrance of Horse Guards where one can see mounted sentries of the Household Cavalry (1100-1600 Mon.-Sat., 1000-1600 Sun.).

Continue down Whitehall past the Cabinet Office, a huge 19thC structure where the government's Cabinet (Inner Committe) sits. Opposite is the Ministry of Defence. Next on the right is Downing St. which is closed to the public. Number 10, the London residence of the Prime Minister, is identifiable by the single protruding lamp over its porch, and it is generally guarded by a policeman. Whitehall ends at the Cenotaph which commemorates the dead of both World Wars. Parliament St. begins here and at the end of it stands the Palace of Westminster, better known as the Houses of Parliament (see **A-Z**) and the clock tower known as Big Ben. See **A-Z**.

Walk round Parliament Square and turn left into Broad Sanctuary. Ahead is Westminster Abbey (see **CHURCHES, A-Z**). Cross over to Storey's Gate and on up to Horse Guards Rd. At the entrance to King Charles St. are the Cabinet War Rooms, Churchill's WW2 underground command centre (1000-1750; £3.00, child £1.50). Cross into St James's Park (see **PARKS**) and walk round the lake. Cross over the bridge, go into the Mall, and on to Buckingham Palace (see **SIGHTSEEING, A-Z**). Visit the Queen's Gallery (see **ART GALLERIES**) or see the royal carriages in the Mews (1400-1600 Wed. and Thurs.; £1, child 50p) before walking up Constitution Hill and across Hyde Park Corner to reach Apsley House (see **A-Z**) on the corner of Hyde Park (see **PARKS, A-Z**). Finish at Hyde Park U.

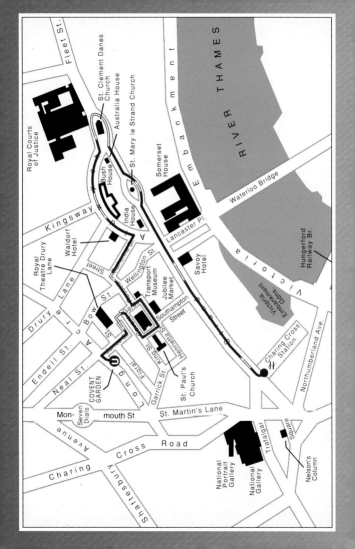

Covent Garden

Begin at Charing Cross Station.

Turn right out of the forecourt and walk up The Strand past the Adelphi and Vaudeville Theatres and Southampton St. which leads directly to Covent Garden. Further along on the right, down a short lane, is the entrance to the Savoy. The present Savoy Hotel was constructed in 1889 on the site of the Earl of Savoy's 13thC palace. Further along is Simpson's, a traditional English restaurant (see **RESTAURANTS**).

Cross over the approach road to Waterloo Bridge to reach Somerset House. Constructed on the site of a former Tudor palace, this 18thC building contains government offices. Its upper floors are intended to house the art collection of the Courtauld Institute (see **ART GALLERIES**). Carry on past King's College and the Baroque church of St Mary-Le-Strand, then cut diagonally across The Strand past St Clement Danes, the church of the RAF, and on to the Royal Courts of Justice with their ornate Gothic facade. The Strand ends at this point and Fleet St. begins. At the east end of the Law Courts is the Temple Bar monument which marks the boundary between Westminster and the City of London. To cross this point, traditionally, the reigning monarch has to be met by the Lord Mayor of London.

Turn back and go onto the crescent of Aldwych. On the opposite side are Australia House, Bush House (home of the BBC World Service) and India House. Cross over Kingsway, then continue past the Waldorf Hotel before turning right into Catherine St. and on up to the Royal Theatre, Drury Lane (see **THEATRES**). Turn left into Russell St. To the right is Bow St. and the Royal Opera House (see **CULTURE**). Ahead is Covent Garden, formerly a market for fruit, vegetables and flowers, transferred to Nine Elms (near Vauxhall) in 1974. The old market buildings were converted into a shopping mall in 1980 (see **SHOPPING AREAS**). Around the pedestrian precinct one passes the Transport Museum (see **MUSEUMS**), Jubilee Sports Hall and the Jubilee Market (see **MARKETS**).

On the far side of the square is St Paul's Church, known as the 'actors' church', designed by Inigo Jones in 1633 (the first Punch and Judy Show seen in Britain was performed in front of it). Continue up James St. to finish at Covent Garden U.

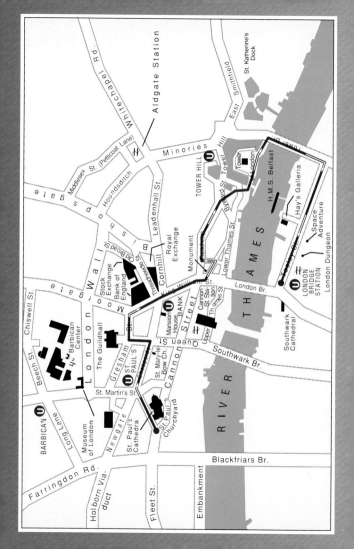

The City

Begin at St Paul's Cathedral (see **CHURCHES**, **A-Z**).

After exploring the cathedral head across Paternoster Sq and carry on down to St Paul's U. Follow Cheapside towards the steeple of St Mary-Le-Bow, another Wren design (1683). Cross over Cheapside and turn left into Kingly St., past Gresham St. and carry on past the church of St Lawrence Jewry, built on the site of the Jewish quarter in the 17thC. Ahead is the Guildhall, seat of the City of London's local government. The Great Hall is open to visitors except when council meetings are in progress. There is also a Clock Museum in the Library (entrance on Aldermanbury round the corner).

Turn left down Gresham St. then follow Princes St. past the Bank of England along to Bank U. On the left is the classical edifice of the Royal Exchange (1842-4) and, ahead on the right, Mansion House, official residence of the Lord Mayor of London (not open to the public). Go under the subway and up into King William St., past the church of St Mary Woolnoth (1716-24), an unusual design by Wren's notable pupil, Nicholas Hawksmoor, and under the next subway to Monument U.

Turning first left into Monument St. leads you to the Monument commemorating the Great Fire of London in1666 (see **SIGHTSEEING**). Turn left into Pudding Lane, site of the bakehouse where the Great Fire started. Turn right into Eastcheap and carry on to the next subway which leads straight on to the Tower of London (see **SIGHTSEEING**, **A-Z**). After exploring the Tower buildings and their treasures, head back to Tower Hill U or visit St Katherine's Dock for some refreshments at the Dickens Inn.

Alternatively, cross Tower Bridge along the walkway gantries high above the river (see **SIGHTSEEING**), then turn right over the bridge into Tooley St. Walk along Tooley St. and into Battlebridge Lane which leads to Hay's Galleria, a converted warehouse with some interesting shops. This road also leads to HMS Belfast (see **MUSEUMS**). On the opposite side of Tooley St. is the London Dungeon (see **CHILDREN**), a horror museum illustrating macabre historical events. Cut across London Bridge to Southwark Cathedral (see **CHURCHES**). Turn left down Borough High St. to the George Inn (see **PUBS**) and finish the walk at London Bridge U.

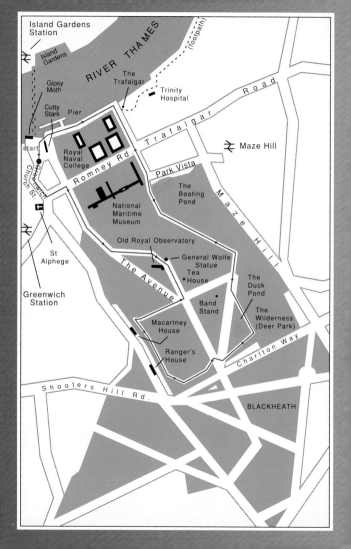

Greenwich Park

Eight km from central London. Train from Charing Cross to Greenwich or Maze Hill (30 min) or Docklands Light Railway (DLR) link from Tower Gateway to Island Gardens (30 min), then a 10-min walk through the foot tunnel. Alternatively travel by boat from Westminster Pier (45 min), Charing Cross Pier (30 min) or Tower pier (20 min). Begin at Greenwich Pier and board the Cutty Sark, a beautiful example of a 19thC tea clipper (1000-1800 Mon.-Sat., 1200 Sun.; £1.40, child 70p). You can also visit Gipsy Moth IV, the vessel which Francis Chichester sailed single-handed round the world in 1966-7 (1000-1800 Mon.-Sat.; 30p, child 20p).

To the left is the entrance to the Royal Naval College with its Painted Hall which is open to the public. Walk up Greenwich Church St., past the tourist office to the entrance of the excellent daily market. Up to the right one can see St Alphege Church, designed by Hawksmoor, and dedicated to the Archbishop of Canterbury who was murdered here in 1012. Turn left into Nelson Rd, right into King William Walk, pass through St Mary's Gate into the Park. Explore the National Maritime Museum which is up on the left. (1000-1800 Mon.-Sat., 1400 Sun.; £3.00, child £1.50 - including access to the Old Royal Observatory).

Proceed up the hill to the Observatory which now houses a collection of astronomical instruments. Outside one can straddle the Greenwich Meridian. Up on the roof the timeball (a signal to Thames shipping) falls at 1300 each day. Follow Blackheath Av to the tearoom where you can stop for refreshment after your climb up the hill. Turn right and head for Macartney House (closed to the public), the family home of General Wolfe who left from here for Quebec in 1759. His statue stands close to the Observatory. Turn left and walk up to the Ranger's House. Built in 1688, it is home to the Suffolk Collection of Jacobean portraits (admission free).

Go back across the park to the area known as the Wilderness. Here are squirrels, ducks and deer, and colourful flowerbeds in summer. Head down the hill towards the gate at Park Row, down to the Trafalgar Tavern, then left for a pleasant riverside stroll beside the College. The walk ends back at the pier. If you wish, you can take a boat trip from here to the Thames Barrier. See **A-Z**.

Accidents and Breakdowns: If you are involved in an accident exchange personal particulars, insurance policy details, *etc*, with the other person(s) involved. The names and addresses of any witnesses could also be useful, and a sketch of how the incident occurred will help to speed up the settlement of claims. Contact the police (dial 999) if anyone has been injured.

In the event of a breakdown visitors who are members of motoring organizations in their own countries belonging to the International Touring Alliance can summon help from either the Automobile Association (AA) or the Royal Automobile Club (RAC). Both provide a 24-hr breakdown service which is cheaper than contacting a garage. They can be summoned using the emergency telephones which are to be found at regular intervals on motorways. Non-members must pay a surcharge for the use of their services. For more details contact the Royal Automobile Club, 89 Pall Mall, SW1, tel: 839 7050 (**U** Piccadilly Circus) or the Automobile Association, Fanum House, Leicester Square, WC2, tel: 891 1400 (**U** Leicester Square).

Accommodation: As you would expect, accommodation is most expensive in the west and south west of the city where many of the top quality hotels are located. More modest, but comfortable, hotels can be found around Victoria, Kensington, Bayswater and Bloomsbury. Demand for accommodation outstrips supply and reservations in advance (in writing, or by telephone) are essential for the high season (usually May to September). Prices fluctuate considerably according to the quality, location and time of year, ranging from £30 to over £400 per night for a room for two people with breakfast. Hotel bills include Value Added Tax (VAT) and service, you should check that prices are inclusive and that 'hidden' extras are not going to creep onto your bill at the end of your stay. Boarding-houses (or self-styled Private Hotels) vary in quality and price, and are usually fully booked well in advance of the high season. The best are in Bayswater, Kensington (Earl's Court), Bloomsbury, and are most numerous around the main railway stations. If you have not arranged somewhere to stay then contact the accommodation service of the London Tourist Board or British Travel Centre (see **Tourist Information**). The LTB also produces a useful publication

called *Where to Stay in London*. Hotels listed with the LTB are graded by a system of 1 to 5 crowns (smaller establishments are indicated by the word 'Listed'). There are hotel reservation offices at Victoria, Waterloo and Liverpool Street Stations and at Heathrow Airport. There is also a variety of booking agencies through which reservations can be made: Hotel Booking Service, 13 Golden Square, W1, tel: 437 5052; Hotelguide, 8 Charing Cross Road, SW1, tel: 836 5561; and Hotel Reservation Centre, 10 Buckingham Palace Road, SW1, tel: 829 1849. See also **Camping and Caravanning**, **Youth Hostels**.

Airports: Heathrow (26 km west of the city adjacent to the M 4 motorway) is the main terminus for arrival in London (tel: 759 2525 for flight information). It is linked to the city centre by Underground Railway (Piccadilly line). Trains run from 0530 to midnight, leave every four to eight minutes and the journey takes about 45 min. London Transport operates a 24-hr express Airbus to the centre which takes from 30 min to over an hour depending on the state of traffic on the outskirts of the city. Airbus services usually terminate at Victoria Coach Station although most buses stop at various points in the city. There is also an all-night bus service (N 97) between Heathrow and Trafalgar Square. A taxi will take about 45 min but can cost up to £20. London's other main airport is Gatwick (42 km south of the city) which is linked by rail to Victoria Railway Station. The Gatwick Express operates every 15 min (hourly through the night) and the journey takes about 30 min. There are also regular express coach services to Victoria Coach Station. A taxi will be expensive and it is advisable to ask for approx. cost before hiring. Heathrow and Gatwick are linked by regular bus services.

London's new City Airport is adjacent to the King George V Dock nine km east of the city centre. At present it operates scheduled flights to Paris, Brussels, Amsterdam, Jersey and Guernsey. Tel: 474 5555 for details.

Albert, Prince Consort (1819-1861): German aristocrat who married Queen Victoria (see **A-Z**) in 1840. She commissioned the ornate Albert Memorial in Kensington Gore after the death of her devoted husband, but he is perhaps better remembered by the Natural History Museum, the Science Museum and the Victoria & Albert Museum (see **MUSEUMS 1**, **A-Z**), all founded with the proceeds of the Great Exhibition of 1851, inspired and organized by Albert.

Annual Events: *January*: International Boat Show, Earl's Court. *February*: Chinese New Year (festivities and parades); Cruft's Dog Show, Earl's Court. *March*: Oxford v Cambridge University Boat Race; Easter Parade, Battersea Park; Ideal Home Exhibition, Earl's Court. *April*: London Book Fair, Barbican Centre; 21 Queen's Birthday (gun salutes from Hyde Park and the Tower); Camden Arts Festival, Camden Town Hall, *etc*; 23 (St George's Day) Shakespeare's Birthday Service, Southwark Cathedral. *May*: Opening of the Royal Academy Summer Exhibition (until August); Covent Garden Proms, Royal Opera House; Chelsea Flower Show, Royal Hospital, Chelsea, SW3. *June*: Trooping the Colour, Horse Guards Parade; Wimbledon Lawn Tennis Championships. *July*: City of London Festival; Royal Tournament, Earl's Court; Henry Wood Promenade Concerts, Royal Albert Hall; Powerboat racing to Calais and back, Tower Bridge. *August*: Carnival, Notting Hill. *September*: 15 Battle of Britain Day (fly-past of aircraft over the city); Autumn Antiques Fair, Chelsea Old Town Hall. *October*: Royal Horse of the Year Show, Wembley Arena; Trafalgar Day (service and decoration of Nelson's Column). *November*: London to Brighton Veteran Car Run; Lord Mayor's Show, City of London; London Film Festival, National Film Theatre, South Bank; State Opening of Parliament by the Queen; 11 Festival of Remembrance, Royal Albert Hall; (Sunday nearest 11th) Remembrance Day Service, Cenotaph, Whitehall. *December*: International Show-Jumping Championships, Olympia; 26-28 Carol Services, Westminster Abbey, St Paul's, Southwark Cathedral, Trafalgar Square; 31 midnight New Year celebrations in Trafalgar Square.
A diary of *London Events and Entertainments* is obtainable (free) from the London Tourist Board information centres. See **Tourist Information**.

Antiques and Auction Houses: Bond Street and Knightsbridge have large numbers of expensive antique shops. At the other end of the scale, many of London's markets contain stalls selling bric-a-brac, coins, stamps and memorabilia. These markets are of interest to the serious collector as well as to the casual visitor (see **MARKETS**). In addition, there are indoor antique-markets along the King's Road and in Kensington High Street. Equally interesting are the sales at London's famous auction houses in the West End: Christies in King Street, Phillips in Blenheim Street and Sotheby's in New Bond Street (viewings and auctions open to the public 0900-1630 Mon.-Fri.). Check the regulations for importing antiques into other countries.

Apsley House: Located at Hyde Park Corner, this house designed by Robert Adam is known as 'No. 1 London' because it was the first residence a traveller coming from the west would encounter. The building now houses the Wellington Museum (1000-1800 Tues.-Thurs. & Sat., 1430-1800 Sun. £2.00, child £1.00) which contains paintings, silverware, porcelain and relics associated with the Duke of Wellington (see **A-Z**), who lived here from 1817. See **WALK 1**.

Baby-sitters: Most larger hotels operate a baby-listening service. The following agencies provide a baby-sitting or nanny service: Baby-sitters, 271 King Street, W8 (tel: 741 5566); Childminders, 9 Paddington Street, W1 (tel: 935 9763); Universal Aunts, 250 King's Road, SW, (tel: 351 5767). These usually charge an hourly rate plus a registration fee - check details before booking. In addition, Junior Jaunts of 4a William Street, SW1 (tel: 235 4700) will take small groups of children on sightseeing trips around the city.

Baker Street: Runs north to south between Regent's Park and Portman Square. No. 221b was the supposed address of Sherlock Holmes, the fictitious amateur detective created by Sir Arthur Conan Doyle (1859-1930). The site is occupied by a branch of a major building society, but artefacts associated with the great detective can be found in a small museum above the Sherlock Holmes pub behind Charing Cross (see **PUBS**).

Banks: Banks are open 0930-1530 Mon.-Fri. (1500 in the city) and

close Sat., Sun. and Public Holidays. Some West End branches open late Thurs. (until 1800 or 2000) and Sat. morning (0930-1230). Heathrow and Gatwick (see **Airports**) have 24-hr banking and money-changing facilities. The main branches of the major English banks are: Barclays, 54 Lombard Street, EC3; Lloyds, 71 Lombard Street, EC3; Midland, Poultry, EC2; and National Westminster, 41 Lothbury, EC2. Most branches have *bureaux de change*. See **Currency**, **Traveller's Cheques and Credit Cards.**

Barbican: The Barbican Arts Centre is the largest of its kind in western Europe. Completed in 1982, its rather confusing internal layout contains a concert hall (headquarters of the London Symphony Orchestra), two theatres (where the Royal Shakespeare Company is based), an art gallery (one of the biggest in London, exhibiting mainly 20thC and contemporary work), three cinemas, a library, conference facilities and two restaurants. Free concerts and exhibitions are held daily in the foyer. See **CULTURE**.

Bicycle and Motorbike Hire: An ideal way of seeing London despite the heavy traffic. Motorcycles should be parked safely and securely locked. To hire one you will require a clean driving licence. Many companies only hire to those 21 years of age or over. Rates per day: mopeds from £10.95; motorcycles from £19.95; bicycles from £3.00-£4.00. There are also reduced weekly rates. Bike UK Ltd, Lower Robert Street, WC2, tel: 839 2111 (U Covent Garden); Chelsea Bicycles, 13/15 Park Walk, SW10, tel: 352 3999 (U S Kensington); Dial-a-Bike, 18 Gillingham Street, SW1, tel: 828 4040 (U Victoria); On Your Bike, 52/54 Tooley Street, SE1, tel: 378 6669 (U London Bridge); Porchester Cycles, 8 Porchester Place, W2, tel: 723 9236 (U Marble Arch); Scootabout, 59 Albert Embankment, SE1, tel: 582 0055 (BR/U Vauxhall).

Big Ben: The large bell, weighing over 13 tons, which sounds from the clock tower at the north end of Westminster Palace (House of Commons end). Its chime is known all over the world. The name 'Big Ben' is popularly (but inaccurately) applied to the clock tower itself.

Blenheim, Palace of: This magnificent palace was the gift of a grateful Parliament to John Churchill, Duke of Marlborough, for his defeat of the French at the battle of Blenheim (1704). Marlborough's descendant and biographer, Sir Winston Churchill (see **A-Z**) was born here in 1874 and is buried in the nearby family cemetery at Bladon.

Blue Plaques: In London you will see round blue plaques at certain sites to commemorate famous people, buildings or events. Plaques are awarded by the Historic Buildings and Monuments Commission to suitable candidates whose work deserves recognition (and who must have been born at least 100 years previously and deceased for at least 20 years). To date there are over 400 of them dotted throughout the city.

Boat Services: One of the best ways to see London is by motor-launch on the Thames. In summer there are regular services operating from Westminster, Charing Cross and Tower piers. Downstream services run to the Tower of London, and then on to Greenwich and around the Thames Flood Barrier. There are also upstream services from Westminster Pier to Kew, Richmond and Hampton Court. There

are also regular lunchtime and evening cruises with discos, music-hall entertainment and dinner-dances. Check details of all cruises by phoning the Riverboat Information Service operated by the London Tourist Board (tel: 730 4812).

London's lesser known waterways are the Regent's and Grand Union canals. They are well worth exploring, either by foot or by taking a gentle cruise on a canal narrow-boat. Several companies operate leisure trips along Regent's Canal from Little Venice through Regent's Park to Camden Lock (daily in summer, weekends only in winter). Contact: Jason's Trip, 60 Blomfield Road, W9, tel: 286 3428; Jenny Wren Cruises, 250 Camden High Street, tel: 485 4433; London Waterbus Company, Camden Lock, NW1, tel: 482 2550. Advance booking is advisable.

Brighton: The attractions of Brighton are as numerous as the antique shops in The Lanes, but you should also visit the Pavilion, the extravagant love nest of the eccentric Prince Regent (George IV) and Mrs Fitzherbert, with its Indian exterior and its lavish Chinese interiors.

Other attractions include an aquarium, a dolphinarium and two toy museums, one in Brighton and one in Rottingdean. Train from Victoria.

British Museum and Library: The British Museum is one of the richest and largest in the world. The collection was originally centred around the geological and zoological items bequeathed to the nation by Sir Hans Sloane in 1753. The magnificent building, with its austere classical facade, was designed by Sir Robert Smirke and built in 1823-47. It would be impossible to view all the exhibits in one visit as they include Greek antiquities, Egyptian and Oriental artefacts, displays covering prehistoric, Roman and medieval Britain, printed books, manuscripts and drawings. Notable among the treasures are the controversial Elgin Marbles, the Rosetta stone (which provided the key to deciphering hieroglyphics), two original copies of the *Magna Carta*, Sumerian antiquities (3500-1500 B.C.) from the city of Ur, and objects from Roman and Anglo-Saxon Britain including the Sutton Hoo and Mildenhall treasures. To assist visitors there are guided tours in various languages. Every hour, on the hour, there are brief conducted visits to the British Library to see the huge circular reading-room and its magnificent dome. See **MUSEUMS 1**.

Buckingham Palace: Originally built in 1705 as the town residence for the Duke of Buckingham. In 1824 George IV commissioned John Nash to remodel the building, but the new palace did not become the official home of the reigning sovereign until 1837 when Queen Victoria took up residence after her coronation. The front of the building looks out over a 40-acre private garden, the back faces the Mall and overlooks the forecourt where the ceremony of Changing the Guard attracts large crowds in summer (every morning at 1130 and alternate days in winter). Although the state apartments (which include the Throne Room, State Ballroom and Picture Gallery) are closed to visitors, works from the royal collections are displayed in the Queen's Gallery on the south side of the palace (see **ART GALLERIES**). In the Royal Mews (further down Buckingham Palace Road) are displayed the Queen's coaches, including the gold carriage used on state occasions. See **SIGHTSEEING 1**.

Bus Services: London Transport's (LT) bus network covers the whole of the city and extends well into the suburbs. The red buses serving the central routes are frequent, but are often delayed by heavy traffic, and get very crowded during the 'rush hours'. Buses usually run 0630-2400 on most routes, and there are a number of all-night services. Fares vary with destination. In addition to buying tickets on board from the driver or conductor, visitors to London can obtain various special daily tickets such as the 'Red Bus Rover' which allows unlimited travel on all city buses, and bus passes are available for periods ranging from one week to a year. Details of fares and passes, plus information on bus numbers and routes, are displayed on a free map available from LT Information Centres and Tourist Information Centres. You can also contact London Transport 's 24-hour Travel Information Service, tel: 222 1234.

Green Line Coaches serve the south east and are ideal for day-trips out of London. The main departure point for these is Eccleston Bridge near Buckingham Palace Road, Victoria, SW1. National Express is the main operator for coach services outside London. Ticket and service details can be obtained from the main departure terminal at Victoria Coach Station. See **City Tours**, **Tourist Information**.

Cameras and Photography: Cameras can be obtained from specialist dealers as well as retailers selling electrical and hi-fi goods (see **SHOPPING**). In addition, large chain-store chemists such as Underwoods and Boots sell photographic equipment as well as offering film developing services. There are a great many instant processing outlets prominently situated throughout the city offering a rapid service.

Camping and Caravanning; There are no camping sites or caravan parks in central London and camping is strictly prohibited in London's parks. There are a variety of campsites on the outskirts of the city and the London Tourist Board produces a free list giving details of their locations, costs, facilities and opening times.

Canterbury: The cathedral here, the centre of the Anglican church, was founded in AD 605. The present church was begun in 1067 and has been a place of pilgrimage since Henry II's knights rid him of his 'turbulent priest' by murdering Archbishop Thomas á Becket in the cathedral. Bomb damage in the war revealed the Stone Age, Roman and Saxon stages of the city's development, and you can still see almost all of the medieval city walls. Train from Charing Cross or Victoria.

Car Hire; Most of the major car hire companies have offices at the airports and at some railway stations. The minimum age requirement varies from company to company, but, generally speaking, a driver must be over 21 and the holder of a clean driving licence for at least one year. The company will advise on insurance cover. The LTB publishes a free list of car hire companies in London, but only those registered with the tourist board are included. The Yellow Pages telephone directory (available at Post Offices) lists other London-based companies. See **Driving**.

Chelsea: This fashionable residential district on the north bank of the Thames has always been popular with writers and artists. This Bohemian heritage is clearly reflected in the wealth of blue plaques along Cheyne Walk commemorating the various personalities who have lived in the area. The town houses have splendid Palladian facades and Lindsay House at nos. 95-100 is a particularly fine example of the style, as is no. 24 Cheyne Row (off Cheyne Walk), the house where the writer Thomas Carlyle (1795-1881) lived from 1834 until his death (1100-1700 Wed.-Sun. Apr.-Oct. Free.). Adjacent to Cheyne Walk is the elegant Royal Hospital, designed by Christopher Wren (see **A-Z**) and its peaceful gardens, where the Chelsea Flower Show is held each May. You can visit the Museum, Chapel and the Great Hall with its panelled walls (1000-1200,1400-1600 Mon.-Sat., 1400-1600 Sun.). Chelsea is also home to the fashionable shops of the King's Road. Don't miss the newly renovated Michelin House in Fulham Palace Road, a triumph of Art Deco style, converted into an entertainment and shopping centre.

Chemists: Chemists open during normal shopping hours (0930-1730). As well as filling prescriptions and supplying general pharmaceutical goods, chemists also sell cosmetics and toiletries. Some of the larger chemist shops, such as Boots, also stock records, camera equipment, film, *etc.* Chemists should carry a notice indicating the nearest establishment open on a Sunday. Boots the Chemist at Piccadilly Circus is open on weekdays until 2000.

Children: For information about children's activities throughout the city contact the London Tourist Board's Kidsline, tel: 222 8070 (1600-1800 Mon.-Fri., 0900-1600 during school holidays) as well as consulting their publication *Children's London* (costs £2.25).

Churches and Religious Services: London's historic churches display a wealth of architectural styles (see **CHURCHES**). Main Church of England services are held on Sundays. Times vary, so contact individual churches for details, or see the Saturday edition of *The Times*. City churches hold midday services during the week, but are often closed on Sundays. Music and organ recitals are held during lunchtime in many churches including St Bartholomew the Great, EC1; St James's, Piccadilly, W1; and St Laurence Jewry, EC2. Churches of many other denominations can be found in London and the city's ethnic mix is reflected in the number of Hindu and Sikh temples as well as mosques

(the largest of which is sited in Regent's Park).

Church of England: St Paul's Cathedral, EC4; Westminster Abbey, SW1; Southwark Cathedral, SE1; St Martin-in-the-Fields, Trafalgar Square, WC2. *Church of Scotland*; St Columba's, Pont Street, SW1. *Roman Catholic*: Westminster Cathedral, Ashley Place, Victoria Street, SW1; Brompton Oratory, Brompton Road, SW7; St George's Cathedral, Lambeth, SE1; Church of the Immaculate Conception, Farm Street, Berkeley Square, W1. *Baptist*: Bloomsbury Central, Shaftesbury Avenue (New Oxford Street), W1. *Methodist*: Central Hall, Westminster, SW1. *Society of Friends*: Friends' House, Euston Road, NW1. *Greek Orthodox*: 184 Mare Street, E8. *Islam*: The Mosque, Regent's Park, NW1. *Jewish*: West London Synagogue, 34 Upper Berkeley Street, W1; Central Synagogue, Great Portland Street, W1.

Churchill, Sir Winston (1874-1965): Britain's greatest states-man of the 20thC, and also a soldier, author and orator, as well as an enthusiastic amateur artist and bricklayer. After 40 years of parliamentary service he was entrusted with leading the wartime coalition government in 1940. His oratorical skill and inspirational leadership did much to encourage the resiliance of the British people throughout the war, and many of his stirring speeches and astute aphorisms are familiar to present generations. He served a further term as Prime Minister in the early 1950s. His country home at Chartwell near Westerham (train from Charing Cross or Victoria to Oxted, then bus) is open to the public, as is the family seat at Blenheim. See **A-Z**.

Cigarettes and Tobacco: Sold in newsagents, supermarkets, tobacconists, pubs and at kiosks. The well-known brands are available in packets of 10 and 20. Some places in airports and main stations stay open until late at night. See **Smoking.**

Cinemas: Seats in local cinemas are cheaper than their larger West End counterparts, however, new releases can usually be seen first in the West End. Most performances start at 1430 and run continuously until 2300, although some cinemas show late night films from 2300. Some cinema 'clubs' require membership. Listings magazines such as *Time Out* and *City Limits* and local newspapers provide detailed guides to what's on offer throughout the city, from the latest blockbuster to specialized art films.

City, The: The original 'square mile' of London, the area that the Romans called *Londinium*. The City of London has preserved its own traditions, character and form of local government. Despite the fluctuating economic fortunes of the country as a whole, the City remains one of the world's most important financial centres. Thousands of commuters stream over London Bridge into the area each day to staff the offices of banks, stockbrokers, insurance companies and mercantile houses. Every year a new Lord Mayor is elected by his or her fellow Aldermen and Sheriffs from the Livery Companies and the Merchant Guilds (whose origins date back to medieval times). In November the City thrills to the pageantry of the Lord Mayor's Show, when the newly elected mayor parades through the streets from the Guildhall to Mansion House, the mayoral residence. Visitors to the City should walk through its maze of streets discovering Wren's churches, old pubs and the impressive City Livery Companies' Halls such as Goldsmiths,

Fishmongers or Weavers (although they are not open to the public).
Landmarks include St Paul's Cathedral, the Tower of London, Mansion
House, Guildhall, the Barbican Centre, the Lloyd's Building, the
Temple and Inns of Court, the Old Bailey and the Stock Exchange.
See **WALK 3**.

City Tours: The best way to see the city is from the top of a double-
decker bus: London Transport runs The Original Sightseeing Tour which
departs regularly from Piccadilly Circus, Victoria, Marble Arch and
Baker Street Station. An open-top bus is used in the summer months (1
hr 30; adult £5.00, child £3.00; tel: 222 1234). LT also run an all day
coach tour on weekdays throughout the year (7 hr; adult £28, child
£24; tel: 227 3456). All the major sites are visited and lunch is included
in the cost, coaches depart from Wilton Road Coach Station (near
Victoria). Tickets can be bought on board and advance reservations or
further information can be obtained from LT or LTB information centres.
Many other companies operate interesting tours: Culture Bus Ltd runs a
circular tour of the city which calls at many of London's top attractions
(2 hr; adult £3.50, child £2.00; tel: 629 4999). Cityrama run open-
topped bus tours which depart every half hour from Grosvenor
Gardens, Trafalgar Square and Westminster Abbey (2 hr; adult £5.00,
child £2.50; tel: 720 6663). See **Tourist Information**.

Cleopatra's Needle: Standing on the Thames Embankment near
Victoria, this rose-granite obelisk is 21 m high and weighs 180 tons. It
has no direct connection with Cleopatra (predating her by many centuries), but came from Heliopolis in Egypt, one of a pair erected by
Thothmes III about 1500 BC as a tribute to the sun god. It was gifted to
the UK in 1819 by Egypt, and erected on this spot in 1878.

Climate: The weather is a favourite topic of conversation in England.
There are no extremes of heat and cold: mild winters are followed by
spring showers and sometimes even wetter summers! But, contrary to
popular belief, Londoners do occasionally venture out without an
umbrella. At best the climate is unpredictable, so bring warm clothing
and rainwear whatever the season.

Consulates: *Australia:* Australia House, Strand, WC2; *Canada:* Canadian High Commission, Macdonald House, 1 Grosvenor Square, W1; *Eire:* 17 Grosvenor Place, SW1; *New Zealand:* 80 Haymarket, SW1; *USA:* 24 Grosvenor Square, W1; *South Africa:* South Africa House, Trafalgar Square, WC2.

Conversion Charts:

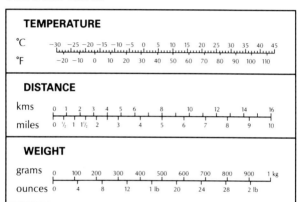

Courtauld Institute Galleries: Samuel Courtauld founded London University's Art History Department and bequeathed his collection, rich in Old Flemish and Italian masterpieces, to it in1931. In 1981 the Princes Gate Collection, including works by Brueghel the Elder and Rubens, was added. The collection is scheduled to be re-housed in Somerset House in 1990. See **ART GALLERIES**.

Crime and Theft: Take the usual precautions and if you have anything stolen, report the theft at the nearest police station.

Currency: The Pound Sterling (£) is worth 100 pence. Silver coins are

5p, 10p, 20p and 50p. Copper coins are 1p and 2p. The new gold coloured £1 coin has replaced the £1 note which is no longer legal tender in England. Notes are £5, £10, £20, £50, and £100. See **Banks, Traveller's Cheques and Credit Cards**.

Customs:

Duty Paid Into:	Cigarettes	or	Cigars	or	Tobacco	Spirits	Wine
E.E.C.	300		75		400 g	1.5 *l*	5 *l*
U.K.	300		75		400 g	1.5 *l*	5 *l*

Dentists: See **Health and Medical Matters**.

Dickens, Charles (1812-1870): The author who described 19thC London in such detail lived for two years at 48 Doughty Street, which has been restored by the Dickens Fellowship with an intriguing kitchen based on that at Dingley Dell described in *The Pickwick Papers*. Dickens died in Gad's Hill in Rochester where there is another Dickens museum.

Disabled: Although some museums, theatres and restaurants provide facilities for the disabled, it is always advisable to phone ahead to request assistance and ascertain any particular difficulties or requirements. The definitive guide book is Nicholson's *Access in London*; alternatively telephone Artsline, the advice service for disabled people in London: (01) 388 2227/8 1000-1600 Mon.-Fri., 1000-1400 Sat.

Docklands: The area downstream from Tower Bridge which was once one of the world's greatest ports. When the last ship departed in

1981 it left behind unemployment, a dwindling population and hundreds of acres of seemingly hopeless dereliction. In July 1981, the London Docklands Development Corporation (LDDC) was given the task of revitalizing this important 55-mile stretch which has featured so strongly in London's history. The area is now being transformed into a thriving commercial, residential and cultural district.

Impressive Victorian warehouses and churches have been restored, pubs with real East End character have been preserved, and a museum is being established to illustrate the historical importance of the area. A new railway line has been developed, The Docklands Light Railway (DLR), to serve the area. It starts at Tower Gateway (close to the Tower of London) and runs east through Limehouse and Poplar. The line ends at Island Gardens and a tunnel under the Thames gives pedestrian access to Greenwich. The LDDC has produced a helpful leaflet outlining different walks with detailed maps which is available (free) from most tourist offices.

Drink: Two very different types of drinks are identified with London: tea and beer. Afternoon tea, complete with sandwiches and cakes, is an

English institution. Although not as important and widespread an occasion as it once was, you can still indulge in this genteel pastime at certain of the larger hotels and department stores.

Beer is enjoyed in another great British institution: the public house or 'pub' for short. No visit to London would be complete without sampling a pint of bitter in the smoky atmosphere of a traditional pub (see **PUBS & WINE BARS**). Some pubs also have revues and theatrical entertainments, or regular live music. Others double as restaurants. Opening hours used to be limited and pubs had to close in the afternoon. However, a recent change in legislation allows them to open from 1100-2300 (2230 on Sun.), although not all pub landlords take advantage of this more liberal regime. Children are only admitted if the pub has a 'family room', garden, or separate restaurant. Alcohol is available in restaurants only when food is also purchased.

Driving: You can drive in Britain with a valid International Driving Permit or a driving licence from your country of origin. Minimum age for driving a car is 17 (16 for motorcycles). Drive on the left and overtake on the right. The speed limit in residential areas is 30 mph (48 kph), 70 mph (112 kph) on motorways and dual carriageways and 60 mph (96 kph) on other roads (unless otherwise indicated). All road regulations are explained in the Highway Code (available from most bookshops). Wearing of seat belts by the driver and front seat passenger is compulsory. Visitors are advised not to drive in London unless absolutely necessary. Conditions are generally chaotic - the latest figures show that traffic moves at an average speed of 8 mph (13 kph), and that congestion is getting worse. The capital's roads were not originally designed for motor traffic so the layout can be confusing for strangers. A road map showing one-way streets is essential. Petrol stations are common in the inner suburbs and central London, many staying open late or all night (see **Petrol**). You will get a parking ticket if you park illegally, for instance on a double yellow line. When cars are judged to be causing an obstruction, they are impounded or wheel-clamped by the police and you will have to go to the nearest police station to pay the fine and have the car released. See also **Accidents and Breakdowns**, **Parking**.

Drugs: UK laws on drug offenders are very tough. This applies both to users and anyone involved in the import and distribution of any drugs, including cannabis.

Dulwich Gallery: England's oldest public art collection. Dulwich is a pleasant south London suburb (30 min train journey from Victoria). The gallery was designed by Sir John Soane and was the first public art gallery to be opened in London (1814). The collection is based around the bequest of Edward Alleyn (1566-1626), an actor who amassed a great fortune , bought Dulwich Manor and endowed Dulwich College. Among the notable Dutch paintings is Rembrandt's *Titus as a Young Man*, and there are fine examples of 17th and 18thC British portraiture, Italian works by Raphael and Veronese, 19thC French paintings and some superb sketches by Rubens. The gallery is located at College Road, SE21, tel: 693 5254. 1100-1700 Tues.-Sat. 1400-1700 Sun. £1.50, child free. Free guided tours on Saturdays and Sundays at 1500.

Eating Out: London offers a vast range of tempting cuisines, from exquisite French and Italian dishes to unusual Japanese, African and West Indian food. Prices too cover a broad range. Price categories in

the **RESTAURANTS** topics are for a three-course meal, with coffee per person. Budget is under £10, Medium £10-20, Expensive over £20. There are large numbers of restaurants around Covent Garden, Soho, the West End and South Kensington, the most expensive being around Piccadilly and Regent Street. Soho, especially, offers an exotic variety of eating places at reasonable prices. For more informal meals and quick snacks, there are many fast-food outlets, including burger bars, baked potato shops, pizzerias and sandwich bars. Many department stores also have reasonably priced eating places. Most pubs and wine bars serve food at lunchtime. There is no official classification for eating places, but specialist publications such as Egon Ronay, Michelin and *Time Out* provide expert guidance to the best, and the worst, on offer. See **RESTAURANTS**.

Electricity: The standard voltage is 220-240V AC. Power sockets take plugs with three square pins; fuses are three, five and 13 amps. Visitors from overseas bringing their own electrical appliances may need an adapter (available from airport shops, and most shops selling electrical goods).

Emergencies: Dial 999 (no coins are required) and ask for Police, Fire Brigade or Ambulance. See **Accidents and Breakdowns**, **Health and Medical Matters**, **Crime and Theft**, **Lost Property**, **Consulates**.

Excursions and Tours: London, at the centre of a vast rail and road network, is ideally placed for day, weekend or week-long excursions into surrounding areas and towns. Ideas and details can be obtained from the British Travel Centre, Victoria Coach Station, or from any travel agent. See **EXCURSIONS**, **Tourist Information**.

Exhibitions and Trade Fairs: Major international commercial exhibitions and trade fairs are held in London at the following venues: Earl's Court Exhibition Centre, Warwick Road, SW5 (U Earl's Court); Olympia, Hammersmith Road, Kensington, W14 (U Olympia); Wembley Exhibition Hall (U Wembley Park or BR/U Wembley Central); Alexandra Pavilion (BR Alexandra Park and shuttle bus service during exhibitions). Yearly programme details and schedules are available from the London Tourist Board. See **Tourist Information**.

Food: The first taste of genuine English cuisine that the visitor to London may experience is the 'Full English Breakfast' available on some hotel or cafe menus. This normally consists of fried sausage, bacon and egg, with perhaps fried tomato, black pudding and even fried mushrooms. However, in these more health-conscious days, 'Continental Breakfast' is usually available comprising anything from tea and toast to coffee, croissant and jam. In fact continental cuisine is far more prevalent than traditional English food, although typical English dishes (enlivened by borrowings from European haute cuisine) such as roast lamb and beef, pigeon pie, rabbit stew, steak and kidney pudding, *etc*, have recently become quite fashionable. Restaurants which specialize in good quality English dishes, however, tend to be more expensive than equivalent establishments serving continental food.

Most pubs, hotel carveries and lower-priced cafés also provide roasts, 'bangers and mash' (sausages and creamed potatoes), steak pie, 'toad-in-the-hole' (sausages embedded in Yorkshire pudding) and other common English dishes at very reasonable prices. If nothing else, traditional fish 'n' chips, whether eaten in the shop or taken away wrapped in newspaper and eaten outside, is one delicacy that all foreign visitors should try. See **RESTAURANTS.**

Greenwich: Situated 10 km downstream from London, Greenwich is famous the world over for the meridian which determines Greenwich Mean Time. The town is also worth visiting for its park, hospital (Royal Naval College), the Old Royal Observatory and the National Maritime Museum, and deserves at least a day to explore its delights. See **PARKS, WALK 4**.

Guides: The London Tourist Board provide officially trained guides (see **Tourist Information**). Various organizations also offer walking tours. Contact: London Walks (tel: 441 8906), Discovering London (tel: 0277 213704) and Citysights (tel: 739 2372).

PRIME MERIDIAN
OF THE WORLD

EAST
LONGITUDE | WEST
LONGITUDE

Hampstead Heath: From the crest of the ridge in the Heath you can see clear across London to the Surrey Downs. This is one of London's favourite places for a day out among the trees, glens, open spaces and pools. Here you can ride, swim, jog, fish, fly a kite, sail a boat or just watch the others enjoy themselves. See **PARKS**.

Hampstead: One of the most attractive 'villages' in London, which has been home to many writers and artists, including Keats, Constable and D. H. Lawrence. Hampstead lies to the north of London 30 min by tube (on the Northern Line). Savour the luxurious surroundings of Fenton House in Hampstead Grove with its sumptuous Regency interior. Also of interest is Kenwood House in Hampstead Lane which houses the superb collection of paintings amassed by E. C. Guinness, first Earl of Iveagh. Summertime concerts are held in the beautiful gardens. Keats's House in Wentworth Place contains mementoes from the poet's occupancy; during his two years there he composed some of his most famous works, including *Ode to a Nightingale*. After a walk around the heath you can enjoy a relaxing drink at one of Hampstead's many famous pubs: The Flask in Flask Walk, named from the era when Hampstead had its own spa and assembly rooms; Jack Straw's Castle, which has a fine view from the top of the Heath and is named after a leader of the Peasants' Revolt; or the Spaniards Inn which Dick Turpin, the 17thC highwayman, is said to have frequented.

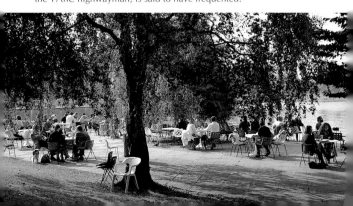

Hampton Court: No British monarch since George II has lived at Hampton Court, but it is perhaps the most beautiful of all the royal palaces. See **EXCURSIONS**.

Health and Medical Matters: Visitors can consult National Health Service (NHS) doctors or dentists, but they do have to pay, so it is essential to take out health insurance before you leave home. However residents of EC countries, or those with similar reciprocal arrangements, will be treated free of charge for illnesses contracted in the UK. Emergency and accident victims requiring hospital treatment are not charged. The following hospitals have 24-hr casualty departments in case of emergencies:

St Bartholomew's Hospital, West Smithfield, EC1, tel: 601 8888.
U St Paul's. General hospital.
Charing Cross Hospital, Fulham Palace Road, SW6, tel: 748 2040.
U Hammersmith Broadway. General hospital.
St Thomas's Hospital, Lambeth Palace Road, SE1, tel: 928 9292.
U Westminster. General hospital.
University College, Gower Street, WC1, tel: 387 9300.
U Warren Street. General and dental hospital.
Moorfields Eye Hospital, High Holborn, WC1, tel: 253 3411.
U Holborn. For eye casualties. See also **Chemists**.

Houses of Parliament: See **Palace of Westminster.**

Hyde Park: The most famous and most popular of the royal parks. The park merges with Kensington Gardens and together they cover some 600 acres which were once the favourite hunting-grounds of King Henry VIII. It was first opened to the public in the 17thC. You can walk round the Serpentine Lake or along Rotten Row (used for horse-riding). On a Sunday afternoon visit Speakers' Corner (U Marble Arch), close to the site of the old Tyburn Gallows. Today large crowds are attracted to a less gruesome spectacle - the soapbox orators voicing their opinions on issues of the day. You will also find the Serpentine Gallery (a small modern art collection), Lido, children's paddling pools and sandpits (May-Sept.), rowing boats for hire (Mar.-Oct.), tennis courts and a putting green. In summer there are regular lunchtime concerts at the bandstand. See **PARKS**.

Insurance: See **Passports and Customs**, **Car Hire**.

Johnson, Samuel (1709-1784): The writer, lexicographer, wit and sage lived at Gough Square during the eight years he worked on his famous dictionary. You can visit the house and see the conditions in which he and his six clerks lived and worked. After your visit you can have a drink to his memory in his favourite inn, *Ye Olde Cheshire Cheese* in Wine Office Court, off Fleet Street. See **PUBS**.

Kensington: A very residential and exclusive district (especially the south), Kensington offers a variety of activities and entertainments for the visitor. South Kensington contains a number of important museums - the Victoria & Albert, Science Museum, Natural History Museum and Geological Museum - as well as the Imperial College of Science and Technology. Shops range from the grandeur of Harrods in Brompton Road, to the antique dealers in Kensington Church Street and the fashionable stalls of Kensington Market in the High Road. Parkland includes Kensington Gardens (see **PARKS**) and Holland Park which contains the beautiful gardens in the grounds of Holland House. The Commonwealth Institute in front of Holland Park holds many interesting exhibitions.

Kew: These beautiful gardens are a must for any lover of trees, shrubs, flowers and herbs. See **EXCURSIONS**.

Knole: Like many beautiful Tudor houses, this was coveted by Henry VIII and confiscated from its owner Thomas Cranmer. It has been owned by the Sackville family for 400 years and they have created a beautiful park which is always open. The house has a fine collection of furniture, tapestries, rugs and hangings. Train from Charing Cross to Sevenoaks and local bus.

Laundry: Larger hotels have their own facilities. Launderettes offer same-day service washes costing about £2.00. Most are open seven days a week. Dry-cleaners offer express services (prices vary according to items cleaned).

Leicester Square: The square was originally laid out in1665 and soon gained notoriety as a duelling ground. It became a public garden in 1874. Statues within the square include marble busts of Shakespeare (a copy of the original in Westminster Abbey) and Hogarth (who lived nearby), and the recently added bronze statue of Charlie Chaplin by John Doubleday. The association with the world of entertainment continues with four large cinemas, the Empire Ballroom and the adjacent Talk of the Town cabaret club. Also located here is the reduced price theatre ticket booth where cheap tickets are sold for available performances.

London Bridge: Until 1749 this was the only bridge over the Thames in London. The bridge of nursery rhyme fame was dismantled in 1968-71 and reconstructed at Lake Havasu City, Arizona, USA.

Lost Property: Enquire at the Police Station nearest to where the loss occurred or at the Metropolitan Police Lost Property Office, 15 Penton Street, W1 (0900-1600 Mon.-Fri.; no telephone enquiries).
British Rail: ask at the Lost Property office of the relevant station.
London Transport Bus and Underground: Enquiries to 200 Baker Street, W1 (0930-1730 Mon.-Fri.; no telephone enquiries).
Taxis: Metropolitan Police Property Office, 15 Penton Street, W1.
Airlines: contact relevant carrier. If loss occurred inside the airport buildings then contact the Airport Police.

Markets: Street markets are part of the fabric of London life and visitors to the city should take advantage of the colourful experiences they offer, and perhaps pick up a bargain at the same time. Two of the most popular at weekends are Camden Lock on Regent's Canal, and Petticoat Lane in Middlesex Street. The former sells quite expensive antiques, clothes, jewellery and crafts, the latter cheap clothing and domestic goods of every description. Brick Lane to the north of Petticoat Lane is even cheaper. During the week Camden Passage is a good spot for antiques, as is Portobello Road where real bargains are a possibility. Kensington Market in Kensington High Street specializes in fashionable new and second-hand clothing. For food and plants try Leadenhall, Gracechurch Street (U Bank), a covered market in the heart of the City. Visitors may also find the large wholesale food markets in the city of some interest: Smithfield, Charterhouse Street (U Farringdon, Barbican) is one of the largest meat markets in the world (closed Sat.); Spitalfields, Commercial Street (U Liverpool Street) sells fruit, vegetables and flowers; Billingsgate on the Isle of Dogs is the principal fish market (DLR from Tower Gateway to Island Gardens). However, please note that visitors cannot expect to freely wander through these wholesale markets. See **MARKETS**.

Mayfair: It is hard to imagine that this most fashionable area was once the scene of riotous and disorderly behaviour. In fact things were so bad that the May Fair, after which it was named, was banned by Royal Decree in the 18thC. The area is now associated with the quality shops of Oxford Street, Bond Street and the elegant Burlington Arcade

(which is still patrolled by a top-hatted beadle), the first shopping precinct in England (1819). More exclusive boutiques are to be found in the South Molton Street pedestrian precinct. Sartorial elegance may be acquired (at a price) from one of the many exclusive Savile Row tailors. The hotels and casinos of Park Lane are world-famous, but for a more informal evening in Mayfair there are many cafes and restaurants around the narrow streets and alleys of Shepherd Market.

Money: See **Banks**, **Currency**, **Traveller's Cheques and Credit Cards.**

Monument: Christopher Wren (see **A-Z**) designed this column to commemorate the Great Fire of 1666. Its height is 61 m, which is the distance from the base to the site of the baker's shop in Pudding Lane where the fire started. The climb up the inside to the top is rewarded with the best views of the City skyline, more changed in the past 30 years than in the 200 before.

Motoring: See **Driving**.

Museum of London: This is *the* museum for those interested in details of the history and social life of London from earliest times to the 19thC city portrayed in the novels of Dickens (see **A-Z**). This purpose-built building was opened in 1976 and is situated close to the Barbican. Of special interest is the Lord Mayor of London's State Coach which is used annually in the Lord Mayor's Show. See **MUSEUMS 2**.

National Gallery: From the relatively humble acquisition of 38 paintings by parliamentary purchase in 1824, the National Gallery now possesses over 2000 paintings, the best collection of European art in the world. Periods covered range from the early Italian Renaissance to the French Impressionists of the 19thC (later works of British and European art are housed in the Tate Gallery) and include celebrated works such as da Vinci's *Virgin and Child with St John the Baptist and St Anne* (cartoon), Ucello's *The Battle of San Romano*, Piero Della Francesca's *The Baptism of Christ*, *Christ Driving the Traders from the Temple* by El Greco, and Van Gogh's *Sunflowers*. The collection was first housed in its present building in 1838, on the site of a former royal mews overlooking the north side of Trafalgar Square. As the collection grew, so too did the building. The dome was not added until the1870s, the latest extension was added on the north west in 1976. Proposed further extensions have met with much criticism and debate over their architectural merit. There are regular guided tours as well as lectures and audio-visual displays. See **ART GALLERIES**.

Nelson, Horatio (1758-1805): Distinguished naval commander and one of the nation's great heroes. He met his death at the Battle of Trafalgar, after masterminding the British victory which prevented Napoleon's invasion barges crossing the Channel from Boulogne to Dover. The whole of Trafalgar Square (see **A-Z**) is a tribute to him. Madame Tussaud's (see **MUSEUMS 1**, **A-Z**) has a sound and vision tableau of the battle and Nelson's death. Other mementoes are in the National Maritime Museum in Greenwich Park.

Newspapers and Magazines: English newspapers fall into three main groups. The popular dailies such as the *Sun* and *Star,* and (on Sundays) the *News of the World* and *Sunday Sport* deal almost exclusively with sex and sensationalism. At the other end of the spectrum are the serious daily broadsheets - *The Times* and *Daily Telegraph* (right-wing), *The Guardian* (left-wing) and *The Independent* - and high quality Sunday papers such as the *The Observer* and *The Sunday Times.* In the middle are tabloids including *The Daily Mirror, Daily Express* and *Today* which strike a balance between serious news and frivolous items on the royal family and television soap opera stars.*The Evening Standard* is London's only evening newspaper and provides good coverage of the capital.
Also worth looking at are the weekly listings magazines, which include *Time Out* (good arts reviews), *City Limits* (more radical standpoint), *What's On* and *Where to Go* (details of night-time entertainments). Most newspaper stands in central London sell American and continental newspapers. Newsagents with an extensive range of foreign newspapers are at: 118 Fleet Street, EC2; 104-106 Long Acre, WC2; and 48 Old Compton Street, W1.

Nightlife: London's West End is the theatre capital of the world (see **THEATRES**) and also provides film fans with a wide choice of cinemas showing everything from popular releases to specialized art movies. The Royal Opera House, Coliseum and Sadler's Wells Theatre offer a feast of delights for lovers of opera and ballet; and there is a regular programme of music concerts and recitals at the Royal Festival Hall, Barbican Centre, and South Bank (see **CULTURE**). For those who just fancy a night out on the town there are numerous pubs, wine bars, nightclubs, discos, cabarets, alternative comedy clubs, and rock, pop and jazz venues to suit all tastes and budgets (see **MUSIC CLUBS, NIGHTSPOTS**). Most pubs close at 2300 during the week and 2230 on Sunday, while nightlife in the clubs and discos extends into the early hours. Some pubs offering live music stay open until midnight. Opening times of clubs and discos can vary, although most close at 0300. The minimum legal age to drink alcohol is 18, but some pubs will only serve those aged 21 or over. Prices vary, but you should expect to pay about £1.20 for a pint of beer and 80p for a measure of spirits in a pub, and three to four times this in a club or disco. In discos, different prices apply depending on whether it is mid-week, the week-end, or early evening. See **What's On**.

Palace of Westminster: This immense Gothic edifice bordering the Thames is officially known as the New Palace of Westminster, the old palace (which was the residence of the sovereign from the 11th-16thC) having been destroyed in a spectacular fire in 1834. Westminster Hall, which survived the fire, was the meeting place of the Great Council of the medieval monarchs, and after 1547 became the seat of the Commons. Part of the the cloisters, St Stephen's Hall and the crypt also survived to become incorporated into the new Houses of Parliament, designed and built by Charles Barry and his assistant Pugin between 1840-60. The porch under the Victoria Tower in the south west corner is entered by the sovereign during the state opening of Parliament. The Clock Tower at the north end houses 'Big Ben' (see **A-Z**), the bell famous for its accuracy and distinctive chimes. It was cast in 1858 and weighs over 13 tons. The House of Lords has a grand Gothic hall with red leather benches. The House of Commons was

destroyed during the Blitz in 1941 and rebuilt in quasi-Gothic style by Gilbert Scott. Up in the Public Gallery you can attend Prime Minister's question time on Tuesday and Thursday afternoons, and at 1000 each morning observe Parliament discuss draft legislation. St Stephen's Porch gives access to Westminster Hall, and in the corner steps lead down to to St Stephen's Crypt, where MPs can hold their weddings and have their children christened. Other rooms of the palace house the MPs' offices and commissions as well as the magnificent library, also designed by Pugin (all closed to the public). See **SIGHTSEEING 1**.

Parking: The streets of London are usually badly congested with traffic, especially during rush hours: 0800-0930,1600-1900. There is a confusing one-way system in the centre and cars (apart from taxis) are not allowed along Oxford Street, Mon.-Sat. 0700-1900. Parking is regulated by parking meters which take 10p, 20p, 50p and £1 coins, usually for a maximum of 2 hr (0830-1830 Mon.-Fri., 0830-1330 or

1830 Sat.). There is no charge on Sun. or on Sat. afternoons in some districts. For sightseeing it is best to park in an outer London area and then travel into the centre by public transport. Hyde Park (multistorey with underpass to Marble Arch **U**) is one of the best car parks in the centre. For more details contact National Car Parks Ltd, 21 Bryanston Street, Marble Arch, W1, tel: 499-7050.

Parks and Gardens: London's parks and gardens are unrivalled, and the city is considered one of the greenest capitals in the world. There are vast open spaces at Hampstead Heath, Richmond Park, Greenwich Park and Wimbledon Common (which remain largely unspoilt and closely protected). The central Royal Parks (Hyde Park, St James's, Green Park and Kensington Gardens), once favourite hunting-grounds, are perhaps the best known and loved of London's parks. Not to be overlooked are the many leafy squares, and even churchyards, which provide welcome respite from the bustle of the modern city. Most parks are free and are usually open daily 0700-dusk. They also offer a variety of recreational and sporting facilities. The National

Garden Scheme, 57 Lower Belgrave Square, SW1, tel: 730 0359 (BR/U Victoria), organizes tours of private gardens. See **PARKS**.

Passports and Customs: A valid passport is required to enter Britain; citizens of the USA, Commonwealth, European and South American countries do not require a visa. Health certificates are only necessary if arriving from Asia, Africa, or South America.Visitors are limited to a stay of six months, and those wishing to extend this period should contact the Home Office, 50 Queen Anne Gate, SW1, tel: 213 3000.

Pepys, Samuel (1633-1703): Much of the personal detail we know about the twin tragedies of London, the Plague in 1665 and the Great Fire in 1666, is due to this dedicated diarist. One of his former houses can be seen in Buckingham Street, behind Charing Cross Station.

Petrol: Petrol is sold in three grades: Four Star, Three Star and Two Star. Unleaded petrol is also now widely available. Most petrol stations are self-service and the instructions on the pumps are easy to follow.

Pets: The British are a nation of pet lovers, but animals and birds have to be placed in quarantine on arrival in Britain as a precaution against rabies. Dogs are held for six months and birds for 35 days. Do not attempt to evade the quarantine restrictions as the penalties are severe. Visits to quarantined animals are restricted. Dogs are not usually allowed in restaurants and food shops (although this does depend on the individual establishment). The London Tourist Board's publication *Where to stay in London* indicates which hotels do not accept animals (except guide dogs).

Piccadilly Circus: A famous London landmark and busy traffic spot at the junction of Piccadilly, Regent Street, Oxford Street, Shaftesbury Avenue and Coventry Street. The circus is named after the *pickadil*, a type of stiff collar fashionable in the 17thC, sold by a local merchant. At night, the area's sparkling neon signs illuminate throngs of revellers

heading for an evening out in the West End. In the centre is a memorial to the Earl of Shaftesbury (1801-1885) philanthropist and reformer, which is topped by the bronze statue popularly known as *Eros* (the Greek God of Love), although the figure is supposed to represent the Angel of Christian Charity.

Police: City policeman wear distinctive helmets and red-and-white arm-bands (head office 37 Wood Street, EC2, tel: 601 2222). Metropolitan police wear blue-and-white arm-bands (headquarters are at the corner of Broadway and Victoria Street, SW1, tel: 230 1212).

Post Offices: You can buy stamps and dispatch letters and parcels at the Post Office. A first-class stamp costs 20p and will guarantee delivery next day almost anywhere in the UK; second-class postage costs 15p but next day delivery is unlikely. Letters marked 'poste restante' and addressed to the Chief Office (see below) will be kept for a fortnight. Proof of identity is required before they will be released.
The London Chief Post Office is at 24 William IV Street, WC2 (off Trafalgar Square), tel: 930 9580. BR/**U** Charing Cross. Open 0800-2000 Mon.-Sat.,1000-1700 Sun.
The Trafalgar Square branch, 22-28 William IV Street is open 0800-2000 daily, 1000-1700 Sun.
Opening times of other main post offices: 0900-1730 Mon.-Fri., 0900-1230/1300 Sat. Smaller post offices in the suburbs close at lunchtimes. See also **Telephones.**

Public Holidays: New Year's Day, Easter Monday, first and last Monday in May, last Monday in August, Christmas Day and Boxing Day. If any of these fall on a Saturday or Sunday, then the following Monday becomes a holiday.

Public Toilets: You will find them in department stores, stations (main stations have 'super loos' with showers, shaving sockets and baby-changing facilities), pubs and restaurants as well as in certain main streets. Coin-operated toilets can be found in Leicester Square, Victoria Street and Soho.

Railway Services: The main railway stations are linked by Underground and bus services and are as follows: *Charing Cross*, terminus of the Southern Region. *Euston*, terminus of services for the North Midlands, North Wales, North-West England and Scotland (Glasgow). *Fenchurch Street*, terminus for the Eastern Region including Docklands. *King's Cross*, terminus for East and North-East England and Scotland (Edinburgh). *Liverpool Street*, terminus for East Anglia and Essex. *London Bridge*, terminus for the Southern Region. *Marylebone*, terminus for the Western Region. *Paddington*, terminus for West and South-West England, South Midlands and South Wales. *St Pancras*, terminus for the North Midlands. *Victoria*, terminus for South and South-East England and Gatwick. *Waterloo*, terminus for the Southern Region for services to the West of England.

London Transport 'Bus Link' connects Waterloo with Euston, St Pancras, and King's Cross Stations. Special 'Red Arrow' buses also link Waterloo and Liverpool Street Stations (Bus 502) and Waterloo and Victoria Stations (Bus 507).

Generally speaking, suburban trains run 0600-2400 Mon.-Sat., 0700-2330 Sun. Times and details of services are available from passenger information services in local stations, or from the British Rail Travel Centre where you can also buy rail tickets and make advance reservations: British Travel Centre, 4 Regent Street, SW1, tel: 730 3400 (U Piccadilly Circus), open 0900-1830 Mon.-Fri., 1000-1600 Sat.-Sun. (later in summer). Tickets can be bought at any of the other main stations. Fares are calculated by distance and it is cheaper to travel off-peak when you can buy a cheap day-return (after 0930 Mon.-Fri. or any time at the weekends). First-class fares are usually double the ordinary fare. Tickets can be purchased to cover transfers to the London Underground. There are a full range of saver tickets, which you should enquire about, especially if you are travelling a long distance. Children under 5 travel free and 5-16 year olds travel half price.

For details of the Dockland Light Railway (DLR) see **Docklands**.

Regent's Park: Surrounded by the splendid terraced houses of Park Crescent, Park Square, and York, Chester and Cumberland Terraces, Regent's Park is still as Nash designed it in 1820. The Outer Circle follows the circumference of Regent's Park from the Grand Union Canal and the Zoological Gardens in the north, to Clarence Gate and Park Square in the south.

The Inner Circle gives access to Queen Mary's Gardens, where Shakespeare's plays are performed in the open-air theatre during summer evenings. Visitors to the park can stroll through the gardens, hire a boat on the lake, or sit on one of the deck chairs provided and watch the bird life in comfort. See **PARKS**.

Richmond Park: There is so much space here in the largest of all the royal parks you can always manage to be absolutely alone either watching the deer, riding, walking or just lying on the grass. See **PARKS**.

Runnymede: In a meadow by the Thames near Egham in Surrey, a granite pillar protected by a dome donated by the American Bar Association marks the spot where the *Magna Carta* was signed in 1215. Nearby is a memorial to all the Commonwealth airmen killed in WWII who have no known grave, and another to President Kennedy. Train from Waterloo or Paddington, or Green Line bus.

St Paul's Cathedral: This masterpiece by Christopher Wren (see **A-Z**) is the third church to be built on this site (1675). It was the first domed church to be built in England, and was inspired by St Peter's in Rome. Inside one can see the monuments to the Duke of Wellington (see **A-Z**), Lord Leighton, Samuel Johnson (see **A-Z**) and Joshua Reynolds. Features include the choir, with a magnificent organ, and splendid stalls sculpted by Grinling Gibbons in 1690. On the south aisle of the choir stands the monument to the metaphysical poet John Donne, Dean of St Paul's 1620-31, which is the only statue belonging to the old cathedral to have survived the Great Fire of 1666 completely intact. At the corner of the choir and the south transept is the entrance to the crypt, which contains the tombs of famous figures including the Duke of Wellington, Horatio Nelson (see **A-Z**), Turner, Reynolds and Wren himself, and which also contains the London Diocese Treasury (1000-1600 Mon.-Fri., 1100-1600 Sat., Apr.-Sept. 1000-1500 Mon.-Fri., 1100-1500 Sat., Oct.-Mar.). From the south transept stairs lead up to the Whispering Gallery (opening times as for the crypt). Here there are breathtaking views of the dome murals and the choir. Visitors can also experience for themselves an amazing acoustic phenomenon which allows the slightest whisper to be heard at the opposite end of the gallery. Further up (542 steps!) is the Golden Gallery offering thrilling panoramas over the city and the Thames. See **CHURCHES**.

Science Museum: Founded in 1856 and occupying its present building since 1928, the Science Museum attracts more than three million visitors every year. On the ground floor are exhibits illustrating the history and development of motive power, including early industrial engines and steam locomotives, including Stevenson's *Rocket* (1829) and the superb *Caerphilly Castle* (1923), beautifully evocative of the steam age. There are also displays on the history of road and rail transport, and space exploration. The Children's Gallery allows youngsters to examine and experiment with various scientific displays and models. They can learn about metallurgy and the steel industry, glass-making and, on the first floor, micro-processing. On the second floor there is a fine collection of model ships, and displays covering chemistry, computing and nuclear physics. Exhibits relating to medical history, inven-

tions, photography and the film industry occupy the third floor, alongside the National Aeronautical Gallery, where famous pioneering aircraft are suspended from the ceiling. Finally on the fourth and fifth
floors is the fascinating Wellcome Museum of the History of Medicine.
See **CHILDREN**.

Shopping and Best Buys: London is a paradise for shoppers. The
city offers a bewildering choice, from world-famous stores to unique
specialist shops. Oxford Street, with its array of department stores, is
the most popular shopping area. Fashionable shoppers head for the
exclusive jewellers and designer boutiques of Bond Street, Piccadilly
and Regent Street. Savile Row is famous for its tailors; Tottenham Court
Road is packed with furniture, electrical and hi-fi shops and the second-hand book shops around Charing Cross are a mecca for book-
lovers. Children's clothes and shoes, which are not subject to Value
Added Tax (VAT), books, records and hi-fi equipment are all good value
for the tourist.
Clothes, on the whole, are reasonably priced unless you go for designer
labels. Woollens are also good value, especially from Marks and
Spencer. Hamley's in Oxford Street is the world's largest toy shop,
packed with an extensive range of toys and games for all the family.
Most shops are open 0900-1730 Mon.-Sat., some larger stores open
late on a Wednesday or Thursday until 1900 or 2000. In the City some
shops close all day Sat.
Visitors to Britain can obtain VAT refunds on presentation of their passport, but check that the store operates the scheme before buying anything. Also check whether you will have to pay tax on the goods in
your own country if you reclaim the tax here. See **SHOPPING**.

Smoking: Smoking is not permitted in any part of the Underground,
on the lower deck of a double-decker bus or on a single-decker bus.
British Rail trains have smoking and non-smoking carriages which are
clearly marked. Increasingly, no smoking is becoming the rule in
restaurants, cinemas, museums and art galleries. In fact, the trend is
towards a complete ban on smoking in all public places. See **Cigarettes
and Tobacco**.

Soho: This district stretches from Regent St. to Charing Cross Rd and from Oxford St. to Shaftesbury Ave. The sex shops, saunas and peep shows have now largely been replaced by bistros, restaurants and boutiques. Visit the 17thC Soho Square off Oxford St. near Tottenham Court tube station. South of the square is Greek St., which contains one of the more interesting buildings in the area, the House of St Barnabas (1430-1615 Wed., 1100-1230 Thurs.) a charitable institution founded in 1846. On the other side of Shaftesbury Avenue lies the small Chinatown district, which includes Gerrard St. and Lisle St. Chinatown is brimming with restaurants and oriental shops. See also the lovely St

Anne's Churchyard in Wardour St., overlooked by a beautiful tower, all that remains of the church which was bombed in WW2. Most typical of Soho's streets are Dean St., Old Compton St., Poland St., Berwick St. and Brewer St., which are filled with Italian, French and German delicatessens, old pubs and traditional grocers and butchers. Wardour St. is also where most of the film production companies have their offices. At the north-west end of Soho is Carnaby St., fashion mecca of the sixties, now being refurbished as a quality shopping precinct.

Sports: London provides entertainment for all lovers of sport. Wembley Stadium, Wembley, Middlesex (**U** Wembley Park): Home ground of the England football team and the venue of the FA Cup final. There are organized tours around the ground and behind the scenes on most days. The adjacent Wembley Arena hosts showjumping, tennis, boxing and other major sporting events.

All-England Tennis Club, Church Road, Wimbledon, SW19: The last week of June and first week of July is the time for strawberries and cream and, of course, the Wimbledon All-England Championships. The main building also houses the Lawn Tennis Museum (1100-1700 Mon.-Sat., 1400-1700 Sun.).

Crystal Palace National Sports Centre, Crystal Palace, SE19: Venue for many major athletic events in the sporting calendar. There is also an Olympic swimming pool which is open to the public.

Lord's Cricket Ground, St John's Wood Road, NW8: Cricket, that most English of sports, can probably best be sampled at Lord's on a summer Sunday afternoon. There is a museum (open only on match days) which may help to explain the mysteries of the game.

One other sport associated with everyday London life is greyhound racing. You can visit one of the greyhound stadia in the evening in Catford, Hackney, Haringay, Walthamstowe or Wembley.

Tate Gallery: The Tate Gallery concentrates on 20thC British and international paintings and sculpture. The collection originated from the bequest of Sir Henry Tate, the sugar tycoon, in1892. The British Collection includes rural scenes by Constable, horse portraits by Stubbs, landscapes by Gainsborough and apocalyptic works by Blake. Some of Turner's greatest works have been housed in the new Clore Gallery extension. The Modern Collection encompasses the main 20thC schools and movements. The Tate also organizes exhibitions of contemporary works. The museum's restaurant has an excellent reputation and contains an interesting display of Rex Whistler murals. See **ART GALLERIES**.

Taxis: Look out for the famous black taxi cabs. They can be hailed if the yellow 'for-hire' sign is lit, or hired from taxi ranks (outside the

major stations), or by telephone. There is a fixed charge on the meter (minimum 80p) to which further charges are added depending on the distance covered. Ask what the approx. cost will be if travelling long distances. Additional charges are levied for luggage carried beside the driver, and if the journey begins or ends between 2400-0600. It is customary to give a 10% tip.

Telephones: Public telephones are to be found in most streets, railway stations, pubs, hotels and restaurants. It is much cheaper to use a public phone than one in a hotel room. Payphones accept 10p, 20p, 50p and £1 coins. Booths contain dialling instructions and coins not used are refunded when the receiver is replaced (tel: 100 for the operator, 192 for Directory Enquiries and 999 for emergencies). Cardphones are indicated by a green sign. The minimum cost is £1 for a ten-unit card which is obtainable from post offices, tobacconists and shops displaying the green cardphone sticker. International calls can now be made direct from any phone by dialling the country code and then the number required. If problems occur dial 155 for the International Operator or 153 for International Directory Enquiries. Telemessages have replaced telegrams in the UK and this 24-hr service is available by

dialling the Telemessage Operator on 190 (they normally arrive on the following working day). An International Telemessage service is also available, but only to the USA. BT operates an International Communications Centre at 1a Broadway, SW1, tel: 222 4444 (open daily 0900-2000) for telegrams, telexes and international calls. A similar facility is available at Heathrow Airport Terminals 3 and 4. For information on events in London tel: 246 8041; for children's activities tel: 246 8007; weather information tel: 246 8091; for travel information tel: 246 8021. See also **Post Offices**.

Television and Radio: *Radio:* LBC on 261/1152 kHz or 97.3 mHz - devoted to news and events; Capital Radio on 194 m/1548 kHz or 95.8 mHz - a mixture of news current affairs, pop and ethnic programmes; Greater London Radio (GLR) on 94.9 mHz - news, current affairs and pop music; Radio 1 BBC on 275 and 285m/1089 kHz or 104.8mHz - pop music; Radio 2 BBC on 330 and 433m/ 693 and 909kHz and 88-90.2mHz - MOR music and features; Radio 3 BBC on 247m/1215kHz or 90.2-92.4mHz - classical music, poetry and plays; Radio 4 BBC on 1515m/ 198kHz or 92.4-94.6mHz - news current affairs and plays; Radio London BBC on 206 m/1458 kHz or 94.9 mHz - a mixture of news, current affairs, pop and ethnic programmes. *Television:* BBC 1 provides local, national and international news, light entertainment, documentaries, sport and films, *etc*. BBC 2 covers art and culture, current affairs, *etc*. ITV London is shared between Thames TV and London Weekend Television, and broadcasts news, popular entertainment, sport and films, *etc*. Channel 4 broadcasts a comprehensive evening news programme at 1900, and its schedule is generally slanted towards the arts and minority interests.

Thames: 'Old Father Thames' has always played a major part in London's history. From the newly renovated Docklands (see **A-Z**) in the east of the city to the quiet banks of Richmond, Kingston or Barnes, the river offers many different faces and moods to those who take time to stroll along its banks. The best views are from Tower Bridge, the Monument (311 steps) and St Paul's Cathedral (627 steps). See also **Boat Services**.

Thames Barrier: Opened in 1984 by the Queen, this remarkable engineering feat has been dubbed 'The Eighth Wonder of the World'. Its purpose is to save London in the event of a flood tide. An exhibition and film show at the Barrier Centre explains how it works. The barrier can be reached by train from Charing Cross or by boat from one of the central London piers. Alternatively, you can also add it to your itinerary when visiting Greenwich. See **WALK 4**.

Theatres: Listings of what's on can be found in London editions of the national newspapers, and in *The Evening Standard, Time Out, City Limits, What's On* and *Where to Go*. In addition, the Society of West End Theatres (SWET) produces a free fortnightly *Theatre Guide* which is available at hotels, booking offices and tourist information centres. Tickets can be purchased at the box office or by phone using a credit card. Theatre Booking Agents charge a commission, but can often get seats for shows which are otherwise sold out. Students can get stand-by tickets at reduced prices just before curtain-up.
The SWET ticket booth in Leicester Square (open 1200-1400 for matinees, 1430-1830 for evening performances) sells cheap tickets for available performances and adds a small commission charge. Some fringe theatres and clubs require membership, but visitors can join before the show for a nominal fee. The Fringe box office at the Duke of York's Theatre in St Martin's Lane, WC2, sells tickets for most of the fringe venues. For credit card bookings tel: 379 6002. See **THEATRES**.

Tourist Information: The main London Tourist Board (LTB) Information Centre is at Victoria Station Forecourt, SW1 (open 0900-2030 daily, Easter to October. 0900-1900 Mon.-Sat., 0900-1700 Sun , November to Easter). They offer a very helpful service and provide free maps and leaflets plus an on-the-spot hotel booking service. They also sell theatre, excursion and travel tickets, and provide a list of 'blue badge' official guides trained by the LTB. Details obtainable from LTB Head Office, 26 Grosvenor Gardens, SW1, tel: 730 3450. The LTB also handle complaints (which must be in writing) about hotels, *etc.* Other LTB offices are at: Harrods (fourth floor), Knightsbridge, SW1 (**U** Knightsbridge); Selfridges (Basement Service Arcade), Oxford Street,

W1 (**U** Marble Arch, Bond Street); Heathrow Airport, Terminals 1, 2, 3 Underground Station Concourse (0900-1800 daily).
Other organizations: City of London Information Centre, St Paul's Churchyard, EC4, tel: 606 3030. (0930-1700 Mon.-Fri., 0930-1200 Sat. **U** St Paul's); British Travel Centre, 12 Regent Street, SW1 (0900-1830 Mon.-Fri., 1000-1600 Sat.-Sun. **U** Piccadilly Circus). The Travel Centre combines the British Tourist Authority and British Rail (you can buy rail tickets and reserve seats); it has multi-lingual staff and also provides a booking service for theatre and tour tickets, an accommodation service and a *bureau de change*.

Tower Bridge: One of the most photographed sights in London, this massive drawbridge was built 1886-94 and designed by Sir Horace

Jones and Sir John Wolfe Barry. A glass passageway links the massive Gothic towers (the South Tower is open to the public and has a souvenir shop) and offers splendid views over the river. See **SIGHTSEEING 2**.

Tower of London: It has been a garrison, menagerie, royal residence and prison since it was built by William the Conqueror in 1097. Now it is one of the city's most popular tourist attractions despite, or perhaps because of, its dismal and bloody history. The Tower is guarded by the Yeomen of the Guard (known as Beefeaters) in their distinctive Tudor uniforms. On Tower Green is a plaque bearing the names of some of the famous royal victims of the executioner's blade, including Anne Boleyn (1536), Lady Jane Grey (1554) and the Earl of Essex (1601). The Bloody Tower, built in the 14thC contains the room where the 'Little Princes' were supposed to have been smothered by their uncle Richard III. The Chapel of St Peter ad Vincula contains the remains of many of the Tower's victims ('no sadder spot on earth' according to the historian Macaulay). The Crown Jewels are housed in

the strongroom beneath the Waterloo Barracks (headquarters of the Royal Fusiliers). They include St Edward's Crown, fashioned in gold for the coronation of Charles II (1662) and still used in the ceremony, and the famous Koh-i-Noor diamond (106.5 carats) presented to Queen Victoria in 1850 by the army of the Punjab. See SIGHTSEEING 2.

Trafalgar Square: London's most famous square was laid out in 1829-41 by Sir Charles Barry. Nelson's Column was designed by William Railton (1843) and measures over 167 ft (51m). The colossal statue of Nelson was sculpted by E. H. Bailey. The four couchant lions were designed by Sir Edwin Landseer (1868) and the two ornamental fountains by Sir Edwin Lutyens. On the north side is the National Gallery with a bronze statue of James II in front. The classical church of St Martin-in-the-Fields (1721-6), the parish church of the sovereign, stands on the north east corner. It was designed by James Gibbs. See CHURCHES, SIGHTSEEING 1.

Transport: The quickest way of travelling around the city is by Underground (see **A-Z**). Taxis (see **A-Z**) are more convenient for complicated routes, but quite expensive. The best way to see the city is by bus, as well as regular scheduled services there are many organized sightseeing tours (see **Bus Services**). The city's waterways are not the major thoroughfares they were in the past, but ferry services still operate on the Thames from Westminster, Charing Cross and Tower piers (see **Boat Services**). London is ringed with mainline railway stations with services to nearly every part of Britain (see **Railways**). For arrival into London see **Airports**.

Traveller's Cheques and Credit Cards: Sterling traveller's cheques are accepted in most major stores, but they usually charge a commission. You will get a better rate of exchange at banks. Remember to take your passport as proof of identity when changing money. The *bureaux de change* in the major railway stations (Victoria, Charing Cross and Waterloo) are open late. Beware of the high commission charged by some of the *bureaux de change* - look for an LTB registered sign and ask the rate *before* you change any money.

Credit cards (American Express, Access, Eurocard, Diners Club) are now widely accepted in shops and restaurants, however some stores, such as Fortnum and Mason and John Lewis, only accept their own storecards, or cheques accompanied by a banker's card.

Underground: The Underground (or Tube, as it is universally known) is the fastest and easiest way to travel around the city. Services run from 0530 (0730 Sun.) to midnight, and are busiest during the rush hours 0800-0930/1700-1830. In central London you are never more than a few minutes' walk away from a station. Using your free Underground map, you should quickly learn to recognize which route you should take. There are five fare zones, and the cost increases the more zones you travel through. You must buy your ticket before you begin your journey. They are available from the ticket office or adjacent machine. Keep your ticket because it will be collected at your destination. Under 14s travel at a reduced fare, as do 14-and 15-year olds holding a Child Rate Photocard (available at post offices). Under 5s travel free. Visitor Travelcards, obtainable from tour operators and travel agents in advance, give unlimited travel on the Underground and London Transport buses.

Victoria, Queen (1819-1901): The first monarch to live in Buckingham Palace, Victoria set the tone for the British royal family which continues today. During her 63-year reign London became the centre of the largest empire in the history of the world. See **Albert**.

Victoria & Albert Museum: The V & A contains a superbly rich and varied collection of exhibits covering the decorative and fine arts, displayed in a maze of galleries containing paintings, ceramics, textiles, carpets, costumes, jewellery, glass, furniture and fabrics. The exhibits are arranged in Primary Collections according to style, period and nationality, and in special Study Collections by class of object. At least one day is required to appreciate the full wealth of the exhibits, the highlights of which include medieval European and Islamic art, rich Gothic tapestries, arts of Asia, Raphael's Cartoons (1515-16), and English furniture, costumes, and domestic designs from earliest times to the 20thC. There are regular lectures and tours on different aspects of the collections. See **MUSEUMS 1**.

Wallace Collection: Bequeathed by Lady Wallace in 1897, this is one of the world's greatest collections presented to the state by a private individual. Housed in Hertford House, an impressive 18thC mansion, Sir Richard Wallace's remarkable collection is especially rich in French paintings, furniture and sculptures, but also contains Oriental and European armour and weaponry, English, Spanish, Dutch and Italian paintings and Renaissance bronzes. See **ART GALLERIES**.

Wellington, Duke Of (1769-1852): Distinguished military commander and statesman whose finest moment was victory over the French at Waterloo (1815). The honours and gifts given in gratitude by the people and sovereigns of Europe to Napoleon's conqueror can be seen in the Wellington Museum in Apsley House (see **A-Z**). He was Prime Minister from 1828-30.

Westminster Abbey: Consecrated in 1065 by Edward the Confessor who lies buried behind the altar, the abbey has been the scene of royal coronations for nine centuries, and its very fabric is steeped in English history.
The church is crammed with monuments. The Unknown Warrior, buried just inside the entrance, was brought from France in 1920. The north transept includes graves and memorials to various British statesmen including Sir Robert Peel (1788-1850), W. E. Gladstone (1809-98), and Lord Palmerston (1784-1865). The north aisle contains the elaborate tomb of Elizabeth I. Poets' Corner includes the tombs of Browning, Tennyson and Masefield. There is a memorial to Byron, whose body was refused entry (and is buried in Nottinghamshire) and others to many other writers and artists.
The Chapel of St Edmund includes the tombs of Richard II and Edward III. Also notable are the Cloisters dating from 1298, the vaulted roof in the Henry VII Chapel, the Coronation Chair with the Stone of Scone underneath (taken from Scone Abbey in Scotland by Edward I in 1297) and used for nearly every coronation.

Whitehall: The name of the street that runs between Trafalgar Square and the Houses of Parliament. The name 'Whitehall' is synonymous with 'corridors of power' and this area is the administrative heart of the British government, containing nearly all the major offices of state, including Downing Street, the official residence of the Prime Minister (No. 10) and the Chancellor of the Exchequer (No. 11). Only the Banqueting House designed by Inigo Jones in Palladian style (1619-22), remains from the original royal Palace of Whitehall which was destroyed by fire in 1698. The main hall has a vast ceiling notable for its nine allegorical paintings by Rubens. In the middle of Whitehall is Horse Guards, the official entrance to the royal palaces, where the suitably impressive sentries stand watch. Also of interest are the Cabinet Rooms, Sir Winston Churchill's emergency command centre during WW II (1000-1750 Tues.-Sat. £3.00, child £1.50). See **WALK 1**.

Windsor: After the state rooms and chapels of the castle, visit Madame Tussaud's and the Guildhall, or walk in the Great Park. See **EXCURSIONS** .

Woburn Abbey: You can choose to visit the mansion house of the Dukes of Bedford with its state rooms and priceless paintings, or the animal park in the huge estate. Train from Euston to Leighton Buzzard or Green Line bus.

Wren, Sir Christopher (1632-1723): Before the arrival of the skyscrapers the London skyline was the creation of Christopher Wren. After the Great Fire in 1666 he designed a grid plan of wide streets for London but was thwarted by vested interests. However, he rebuilt 56 of the City churches including St Paul's (see **A-Z**) as well as the towers of Westminster Abbey, Marlborough House, the Royal Hospital, Chelsea, the Old Royal Observatory and the Royal Naval College in Greenwich. Many of his city churches can be seen from the Monument (see **A-Z**), which he designed to commemorate the Great Fire of 1666. '

Youth Hostels: The best hostel is in the grounds of the Commonwealth Institute, Holland Park, Kensington, W8, tel:937 0748.

There are others at: Carter Lane, EC4, tel: 236 2965; 84 Highgate West Hill, N6, tel:340 1831; 38 Bolton Gardens, Earl's Court, SW5, tel: 373 3083; and 4 Wellgarth Road, Hampstead Heath, NW11, tel: 458 9054. Contact the Youth Hostels Association, 14 Southampton Street, Strand, WC2 for more details, or the LTB who will provide information on these and other types of cheap accommodation.

CW00471686

INSIGHT○GUIDES

ALASKA
PORTS OF CALL
POCKET GUIDE

⦿ Walking Eye App

YOUR FREE EBOOK AVAILABLE THROUGH THE WALKING EYE APP

Your guide now includes a free eBook to your chosen destination, for the same great price as before. Simply download the Walking Eye App from the App Store or Google Play to access your free eBook.

HOW THE WALKING EYE APP WORKS

Through the Walking Eye App, you can purchase a range of eBooks and destination content. However, when you buy this book, you can download the corresponding eBook for free. Just see below in the grey panel where to find your free content and then scan the QR code at the bottom of this page.

Destinations: Download essential destination content featuring recommended sights and attractions, restaurants, hotels and an A–Z of practical information, all available for purchase.

Ships: Interested in ship reviews? Find independent reviews of river and ocean ships in this section, all available for purchase.

eBooks: You can download your free accompanying digital version of this guide here. You will also find a whole range of other eBooks, all available for purchase.

Free access to travel-related blog articles about different destinations, updated on a daily basis.

HOW THE EBOOKS WORK

The eBooks are provided in EPUB file format. Please note that you will need an eBook reader installed on your device to open the file. Many devices come with this as standard, but you may still need to install one manually from Google Play.

The eBook content is identical to the content in the printed guide.

HOW TO DOWNLOAD THE WALKING EYE APP

1. Download the Walking Eye App from the App Store or Google Play.
2. Open the app and select the scanning function from the main menu.
3. Scan the QR code on this page – you will then be asked a security question to verify ownership of the book.
4. Once this has been verified, you will see your eBook in the purchased ebook section, where you will be able to download it.

Other destination apps and eBooks are available for purchase separately or are free with the purchase of the Insight Guide book.

MISTY FJORDS
Here, the mists lift to reveal mystical peaks, hidden valleys, plunging waterfalls, and lonely shores. See page 51.

SAXMAN TOTEM PARK
Learn what Alaska Native totem poles have to tell us about families, friendships, and life. See page 51.

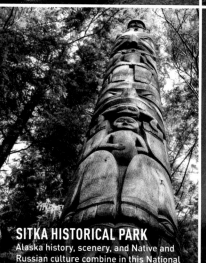

SITKA HISTORICAL PARK
Alaska history, scenery, and Native and Russian culture combine in this National Park adjoining the pleasant town of Sitka on Baranof Island. See page 59.

GLACIER BAY
At least 300 years of glacial retreat have uncovered a wonderful world of sea, ice, and stone. See page 67.

SEWARD SEALIFE CENTER
Get a close-up view of what lies beneath the waves and 'bergs. See page 86.

KENAI FJORDS
Humpbacks, sea lions, moose, bears, soaring peaks, and calving glaciers. See page 86.

PRINCE WILLIAM SOUND
Prince William Sound combines temperate rainforested islands with spectacular tidewater glaciers. See page 100.

SKAGWAY AND KLONDIKE
History is front and center here at the rollicking start of the Chilkoot Trail to the Klondike goldfields. See pages 30 and 73.

DENALI
North America's highest peak overlooks a sprawling wilderness, an Arctic menagerie, and even a few creature comforts. See page 104.

GIRDWOOD/ALYESKA
Enjoy a range of activities around delightful Girdwood or just relax and soak in Alyeska Resort's dramatic setting. See page 101.

A PERFECT CRUIS

Day 1

At sea, northbound from Vancouver, British Columbia

Become familiar with the ship and avail yourself to its amenities, or stroll on deck watching for whales and gazing at the deep forested islands and emerald waterways of British Columbia's portion of the Inside Passage.

Day 3

Juneau, Alaska

Join Alaska's capital city politicians on a lunchtime stroll along the waterfront, and then hop on the tram up Mt Roberts for a hike amid the peaks that overloo this city's incomparable setting. If the weather cooperates, join a helicopter excursion to the vast white expanses of the Juneau Icefield. Alternatively, short jaunt out to Mendenhall Valley will be rewarde with close-up views of Mendenhall Glacier.

Day 4

Skagway, Alaska

Experience the ghosts of Alaska's great Gold Rush with a historic to of downtown Skagway and an excursion to nearby Dyea, where the prospectors provisioned and set off for the Klondike. In the afternoon, ride the rail into the clouds along t narrow-gauge Yukon & White Pass Railway.

Day 2

Ketchikan, Alaska

Welcome to Alaska! Soar in a floatplane over the towering cliffs of the Misty Fjords. Then follow a rewarding excursion to Saxman Totem Park or Totem Bight State Park with a stroll along historic Creek Street or dry out while learning about the temperate rainforest at the Southeast Alaska Discovery Center.

Day 6

~y Strait Point, Alaska

his 'new', ready-made wilderness port for the Tlingit
llage of Hoonah presents a stunning setting, Native
ulture, and the thrill of sliding from mountaintop to
hore on one of the world's longest ziplines.

Day 5

Glacier Bay National Park, Alaska

Enjoy a day shipboard,
ruising through
vondrous Glacier Bay.
Outside, you're treated
o breaching whales,
alving glaciers, wild
orested slopes, and
surrounding icy peaks
hat are higher than any
n the 'Lower 48'. Along
he way, contemplate
hat when early
explorers sailed through
over 200 years ago,
his now vast bay lay
beneath a sheet of ice
,000ft (1,220m) thick!

Day 7

At sea, Hubbard Glacier, Gulf of Alaska

Sailing across the Gulf
of Alaska, take a break
from the range of ship-
board activities and
amenities with a scenic
pause at the 'galloping'
Hubbard Glacier, which
occasionally surges
ahead to turn Russell
Fjord into a lake.
This break affords an
excellent opportunity to
photograph icebergs.

Day 8

Seward, Alaska (and beyond...)

Disembark at Seward
to check out the Seward
Sea Life Center, then
head for Anchorage
to fly home or set off
on a cruise extension
into the wilds. Keep
cruising through Kenai
Fjords National Park,
try your hand at landing
a sockeye salmon,
chill out or take a hike
at Girdwood/Alyeska
Resort, explore Alaska's
'Big City' of Anchorage,
or keep heading north
to experience the
wildlife and wonders
surrounding North
America's rooftop in
Denali National Park.

CONTENTS

◉ **FEATURES**

INTRODUCTION

Alaska: the Great Land, the Last Frontier – more than 580,000 sq miles (1.5 million sq km) that taunted early explorers still challenges modern-day researchers, adventurers, and – especially – vacationers. It also provokes a fascination that attracts cruise-ship passengers who are looking for a non-stop scenic backdrop to a rewarding shipboard experience. Along the way, compact ports of call punctuate a frontier landscape writ large, where rugged pursuits and a respect for the harshness of nature feature prominently in the daily lives of most of its full-time residents.

America's 49th state is so broad, so unpeopled, and so roadless that small airplanes are more common than cabs are in other states. In fact, there are more private pilots than truck drivers and cabbies combined. What's more, men outnumber women (though there is a phrase 'The odds are good, but the goods are odd'). Almost half of Alaska's 730,000 people live in Anchorage and its environs, and most of the rest are concentrated in just a few areas: Fairbanks, the Kenai Peninsula, the Mat-Su Valley, and a few Southeast Alaska ports. The rest of the state is a raw, wondrous, and largely untrampled wilderness, dotted with small outposts and mainly Native villages.

For visitors, the Alaskan experience includes the sheer wonder of finding what hides beyond the horizon or beneath the next wave. No one is able to take it all in and no one ever will. Therein lies the essence of Alaska. Its huge untamed spaces, it has been said, are the great gift Alaska can give to a harried world, and a cruise along its Inside Passage and northward to its extensive Gulf of Alaska coastline will be the most amenable and relaxing way to experience its formidable wonders.

THE NATURAL SCENE

Alaska is a natural paradise of lush rain-drenched forests, soaring peaks, spectacular glaciers, still-active volcanoes, and fragile windswept tundra, as well as 3 million lakes and endless muskeg swamps. Along with a handful of modern towns, there are lots of tiny villages and countless wild homesteads, and even townspeople tend to spend their spare time communing with the land: hiking, camping, hunting, fishing, and buzzing around it on a variety of toys, from ATVs (quad bikes), snow machines, and jet-skis to floatplanes, showshoes, and dogsleds.

By cruise ship, Alaska is a constantly changing panorama that exposes passengers to a wilderness wonderland, a rich wildlife habitat, a wealth of cultural heritage, and – it must be said – sometimes drenching encounters with Alaska's

Columbia Glacier iceberg, Prince William Sound

Tlingit poles at Saxman Totem Park

meteorological proclivities. In other words, for sun and fun, cruise the Caribbean or the Mediterranean, but if you're looking for scenery, adventure, and expansive horizons, Alaska is the right destination.

NATIVE PEOPLES

Alaska has been inhabited for thousands of years by several diverse Native groups, each with its own culture and language. After 1741, however, when Russian explorers and traders discovered that the territory was rich in furs, the lives of the Native peoples were changed forever.

Who were the people who first thrived in such an unforgiving environment? Anthropologists believe the ancestors of the Alaska Natives migrated in several waves over a land bridge that joined Siberia and Alaska thousands of years ago. When Europeans first encountered Alaska Natives in the early 18th century, there were dozens of tribes and languages groups. Today, these first Alaskans are divided into several main groups: the southeastern and southern Coastal Indians, comprised of the Tlingits, Haidas, Tsimshians, and Eyak; the Athabascans of the Interior; the Aleuts of the Aleutian Islands; the Alutiiq of Kodiak Island and environs; and three groups of Eskimos: the Inupiat of the northwest and far north, the Central Yu'pik of western Alaska, and the culturally distinct Siberian Yu'pik of St Lawrence and several other offshore islands.

Of the coastal Indians, the Tlingit, which were excellent navigators, claimed most of the coastal Panhandle, leaving only a small southern portion to the less populous Haidas. In the late 1800s they were joined by the Tsimshian, who emigrated from Canada to Annette Island in the Southeast. The Tsimshian live on Annette Island in Alaska's only federally recognized Indian reservation.

The Athabascans of Alaska's harsh Interior were hunters and inland fishermen. Most lived in small nomadic bands along the region's rivers. If game was scarce, they might travel for days without food; in deepest winter they survived temperatures of –50°F (–45°C) or less, sometimes without shelter or fire. Endurance and physical strength were prized; game was often run down on foot over difficult terrain.

The Aleuts settled the windswept islands of the Aleutian chain 10,000 years ago. Although their location allowed them to harvest the sea's bounty, they also had to contend with harsh and often unpredictable weather, as well as earthquakes and volcanic eruptions. Because of a ready supply of grass in the summer, Aleut women became skillful at basketry – their baskets were so closely woven that they could even hold water. Mats and some kinds of clothing were also made in this way.

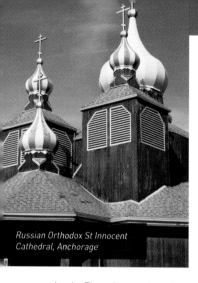
Russian Orthodox St Innocent Cathedral, Anchorage

Close relatives of the Aleuts, Alutiiq peoples, skilled hunters and fishers who (oddly) speak an Eskimo language, settled on the Alaska Peninsula, Kodiak, and parts of the Kenai Peninsula and Prince William Sound.

The Eskimos, who are thought to have arrived by skin boat from Siberia after the Bering land bridge had disappeared, used such boats, called *umiaks*, to hunt larger sea animals. They also used smaller, one-man craft, called kayaks. Women were skilled in basketry and sewing, and the group is also renowned for fine carving, especially in ivory, bone, and baleen (bony plates from the mouths of baleen whales). The *ulu*, a curved women's knife used for cleaning skins and chopping meat, is found in tourist shops today and is appreciated for both its beauty and its utility.

THE RUSSIAN ERA

The story of Russia's invasion of Alaska began in 1741, when two tiny vessels, the *St Peter* and the *St Paul* – captained respectively by a Dane, Vitus Bering, and a Russian, Alexei Chirikof – set sail from Russia. Chirikof met with failure, but the crew of the *St Peter* sighted Mt St Elias on the Alaska mainland and anchored his vessel off Kayak Island, while crew members went ashore to explore and find water. Alerted by these explorers to the riches represented by the fur-bearing marine life and mammals, Russia threw itself wholeheartedly into setting up hunting and trading outposts. For the Native populations, this was an unprecedented disaster. Rather than hunting the marine life for themselves, the Russians forced the Aleut people to do the work for them. Hostages were taken, families were split up, and individuals forced to leave their villages and settle elsewhere.

Around this time, the British began searching for the Northwest Passage, the fabled water route through the Arctic between the Atlantic and the Pacific. In 1778 Captain James Cook sailed north from Vancouver Island, through the Inside Passage and then along the Gulf Coast, to the Aleutians. Along the way, he explored the long, wide bay that would later be given his name: Cook Inlet, which is the site of present-day Anchorage. Then came the Spanish, already well established on the coast of California, who founded the towns of Valdez and Cordova.

⊘ POTLATCH

Historically, in the social organization of the Tlingits and Haidas of Southeast Alaska, a person of power demonstrated wealth by hosting a ceremonial 'potlatch' when he would give away, destroy, or invite guests to consume all his food and possessions. Those who received goods at one potlatch had to reciprocate and better their host at a similar event in the future.

Athabascans also gave potlatches to mark a death, to celebrate a child's first successful hunt, or as a prelude to marriage. Aspiring leaders were expected to host one to give away all his possessions, then prove his prowess by providing for his family for an entire year without outside help.

Meanwhile, a growing contingent of Russians was determined to dig in and keep Alaska's fur wealth for themselves. One particularly ruthless individual, Grigor Ivanovich Shelikof, arrived in Three Saints Bay on Kodiak Island in 1784 with two ships, the *Three Saints* and the *St Simon*. Meeting local resistance, Shelikof responded by killing hundreds of Alutiiq inhabitants and taking hostages to enforce the obedience of the rest. Having established his authority, Shelikof founded the first permanent Russian settlement in Alaska on the island's Three Saints Bay, built a school to teach Russian language and culture, and introduced Russian Orthodoxy. In 1790, Shelikof, back in Russia, hired Alexander Baranov to manage his Alaska fur enterprise and establish the permanent settlement of Kodiak Island.

In 1833, when the British-run Hudson's Bay Company began siphoning off trade, Baranov began to depend heavily on American supply ships, since they came much more frequently than Russian ones. But American hunters and trappers encroached on Russian territory. In 1812 a settlement was reached giving the Russians exclusive rights to the fur trade north of 55°N latitude (the current coastal boundary between British Columbia and Southeast Alaska). Eventually the Russian-American Company also entered into an agreement with the Hudson's Bay Company, which gave the British rights to sail through Russian territory. Pacts were also signed in the mid-1820s that allowed both British and US vessels to land at Russian ports.

By the 1860s the Russians were considering ridding themselves of Russian America, which was too far from St Petersburg to be efficiently supplied and protected. In any case, overhunting had decimated the fur-bearing animal population, and mercantile interest had waned significantly.

A Russian emissary approached the US Secretary of State, William Henry Seward, about a possible sale, and in 1867 the US Congress, at Seward's urging, agreed to buy Russian America for US$7.2 million – just under 2 cents an acre.

THE MAKING OF MODERN ALASKA

People regarded the new possession as a wild land, and before gold was discovered, America wasn't sure what, exactly, it had acquired when it bought Alaska. The interior had been little touched by the Russians, who had stayed in the coastal areas. US exploration, too, had been limited. Whether the US knew what it had or not, the territory still needed to be governed. Unfortunately, back in Washington, DC, legislators were preoccupied with post-Civil War reconstruction. As a result, US Army officer General Jefferson C. Davis was put in charge of Alaska.

Striking gold

By the 1880s, prospectors were pulling gold out of the streams in Southeast Alaska, and Juneau sprang up around a strike of gold-spangled quartz by Richard Harris and Joe Juneau. In fact, the Treadwell Mine on Douglas Island, once the largest in the world, operated from 1881 to 1922 and caused Juneau to be named the territorial capital in 1906.

It was the discovery of gold in Canada's Klondike in 1896, however, that finally made the world take notice of America's northern possession. A wave of fortune hunters clamored for passage to the Klondike, which was most easily accessed via Skagway, Alaska. Then gold was discovered in the beach sands at Nome in 1899, and a combination of fortune and misfortune also led to a gold strike and the birth of Fairbanks in the early 1900s.

Meanwhile, whaling continued well into the 20th century with no regard for overhunting, and American fishing, canning, and whaling operations, as well as walrus hunting, were as unchecked as they were during the Russian era. By the early 20th century, commercial fishing and canning enterprises had taken hold in the Aleutian Islands. Before long, however, overfishing became a serious threat.

World War II

World War II brought new challenges. On June 3, 1942, the Japanese launched an air attack on the US naval base at Dutch Harbor in the Aleutian Islands. US forces were able to hold off the planes, and the base survived the attack, but on June 7 the Japanese landed on the islands of Kiska and Attu, overwhelming villagers and taking them to Japan as prisoners of war. The taking of Attu was the second bloodiest battle of the Pacific theater, after Iwo Jima. Remaining Aleuts were forcibly evacuated to Southeast Alaska, where they, too, were interned, but by the US 'for their own protection'.

WWII had other effects, the most important of which was the Alaska–Canada Military Highway – the Alcan – that was completed in 1942 in just nine months and a cost of US$20 million to form an overland supply route. New military bases also contributed to the growth of some cities. Anchorage almost doubled in size, from 4,200 people in 1940 to 8,000 in 1945, and two other catalysts were just around the corner: statehood and oil.

Gold miners in St Kincaid, 1901

The 49th State

After the war, there was no doubt about Alaska's strategic importance, and the issue of statehood was being taken seriously. In 1955, anticipating statehood, a constitutional convention was called to draft a state constitution. Four years later, on January 3, 1959, President Dwight D. Eisenhower formally admitted Alaska to the union as the 49th state. William A Egan was sworn in as the first governor, and Juneau remained the capital.

It was not long before the young state underwent its first trial. On March 27, 1964, the Good Friday earthquake struck Southcentral Alaska, churning the earth for four minutes. Despite the setback, post-earthquake rebuilding proceeded, including moving the destroyed port of Valdez four miles to a safer location. It wasn't yet known that this small town would figure very

prominently in Alaska's economic future.

Oil riches

In 1968, the Atlantic-Richfield Company discovered oil at remote Prudhoe Bay, and Alaska would be changed forever. The issue of transporting the crude to lower 48 refineries was resolved with the construction of an 800-mile (1,280km) pipeline to the new port of Valdez, where it would be loaded onto southbound tankers.

To pave the way for pipeline construction across Native lands, in 1971, the Alaska Native Claims Settlement Act was signed. In return for aboriginal land claims, Native peoples received title to 44 million acres (18 million hectares) and were paid US$963 million. The land and money were divided among regional, urban, and village Native Corporations.

The cost of the pipeline and related projects, including the tanker terminal at Valdez, 12 pumping stations and the Yukon River Bridge, was US$8 billion, and the first oil arrived at Valdez in July, 1977. During the years of pipeline construction, Anchorage and Fairbanks blossomed into bright, modern cities. The Alaska Permanent Fund, created in 1976, was intended to serve as a hedge against inflation, a fund for the state legislature, and a source of dividends for qualifying Alaska residents. While these decreasing annual dividends have now been capped, every October still sees a mini-economic boom as businesses try to woo residents clamoring to spend them.

Over the past two decades, there has been a steady shift from complete dependence on resource extraction and government employment to service industries. Oil fields on Alaska's North Slope continue as the state's primary economic fuel, but even that has slipped to half of what it was during the late 1980s peak. The timber and commercial fisheries industries have suffered even greater losses.

Tourism boom

Fortunately, in the second half of the 20th century, Alaska discovered another important source of revenue: tourism. The Alaska (formerly Alcan) Highway, built during the war, and the Alaska Marine Highway System, completed in 1963, made the state more accessible than ever before. A couple of major

⊙ THE GOOD FRIDAY QUAKE

At an estimated 9.2 on the Richter Scale, the Good Friday quake remains the most powerful ever recorded in North America, and one cannot understate the damage. Most of the 131 people killed on March 27, 1964, were drowned in the tsunamis that destroyed the towns of Valdez, Seward, Kodiak, and Seldovia.

Along Turnagain Arm, off Cook Inlet, the land dropped 4ft (1.2m), destroying shoreside cabins and drowning entire forests (that are still visible as ghostly remnants). Downtown Anchorage was decimated as buildings toppled and huge chunks of asphalt piled up like shingles, while homes were rattled down unconsolidated slopes. Today, the event is commemorated at Earthquake Park, a popular bluffside stop in Anchorage.

Cruise ship moored in Juneau

cruise lines arriving in the 1970s also added to the tourist boom. Tourism is now very big business, with more than 1.5 million people visiting every year, and while much of the fishing industry struggles to stay in business, increasing numbers of cruise ship passengers are welcomed as a boon to local economies and have sparked local industries in ecotourism and visitor services.

ALASKA CRUISING

Mainstream cruises to (and from) Alaska follow the Inside Passage between the contiguous 48 states or British Columbia, Canada, with extensions across the Gulf of Alaska to the southern coast of mainland Alaska. With the exception of several open expanses – Queen Charlotte Sound, Dixon Entrance, the approach to Sitka, and the Gulf of Alaska crossing – they stay in well-sheltered island-studded passages.

The bulk of Alaska cruising includes two main routes: the Inside Passage only and the Inside Passage plus the Gulf of Alaska. The former is typically a round-trip from either Seattle or Vancouver, but an increasing number are also launching in Los Angeles or San Francisco, with some calling en route at the ports of Astoria, Oregon, or Victoria, British Columbia.

Most Gulf of Alaska cruises, on the other hand, are one-way, either northbound, beginning in Seattle or Vancouver, or southbound, beginning in Whittier or Seward. Although they focus on a Gulf of Alaska crossing and feature pre- or post-cruise excursions further north, they also follow the Inside Passage route and normally take in two or three ports of call in Southeast Alaska. Northbound cruises are the more popular, but an increasing number of people are opting to fly to Anchorage, tour around mainland Alaska, and then slouch homeward on a relaxing southbound cruise.

In Port

With few exceptions, cruise ships moor close to town centers of the ports of call, and it's usually only a short walk from the ship to the commercial district. This means that even if you're not taking an organized shore excursion, you can quickly reach the heart of things on foot. All of Alaska's ports of call include enigmatic waterfronts, with historic canneries, fishing harbors, shops, churches, warehouses, and even former red-light districts. Several of them feature excellent – and sometimes quirky – museums that also provide dry shelter along with their well-presented exhibits.

⊘ NON-TRADITIONAL ALASKA CRUISES

In addition to the standard Inside Passage cruises, new routes are opening up on such innovative cruise lines as Ponant, Silversea, Seabourn, and Crystal. Trans-Pacific cruises run between North America and Japan or the Russian Far East, calling in at Southwest Alaska ports. An increasing number of cruises navigate the Northwest Passage – in the wake of Franklin – between Alaska and Greenland or the North American east coast. Alaska also features in several Bering Sea itineraries, as well as expedition level cruises to Russia's Wrangel Island.

Cruising the Inside Passage and the Gulf of Alaska

The beauty of the mountain, forest, and ice landscapes that connect the ports of call, huddling against near-vertical backdrops, is the main draw, but there's more. The seas hereabouts are filled with marine life, including several whale species, the towns are friendly and compact, and the modern, typically rugged modern Alaskan culture overlays Russian, Tlingit, Haida, Tsimshian, Alutiiq, Aleut, and Athabascan heritage.

Nowhere else in the world is there such a long, sheltered, wilderness waterway where ports of call offer such rustic yet well-organized shore experiences. Today, cruising is not just for the older, wealthy few – Alaska cruise passengers come from all age groups and walks of life, and cruises are designed to suit their different needs. In addition, the virtually hassle-free and entertainment-packed cruise ship environment is particularly attractive to families. And, of course, careful budgeters will find the value for money is undeniable.

There was a time when just getting to Alaska was an adventure, and Alaska cruising has come a long way since the 1870s – shortly after the US purchase of Alaska from Russia in 1867. The first tourists booked steamship passage to Alaska based on rumors of 'unparalleled scenery', and these early cruisers were able to rub elbows with Gold Rush prospectors, opportunistic shysters, and US military operations making their presence known among Alaska Natives.

Since those days, the worldwide cruising industry has grown enormously. The concept hasn't changed much but amenities have been vastly improved, refined, expanded, and packaged. Companies operating large ships (loosely defined as those carrying between 2,500 and 5,400 passengers) now dominate the market, but mid-range and smaller vessels (carrying fewer than 700 passengers) also have a place and

Sailing through the Wrangell Narrows to Petersburg, Southeast Alaska

are able to navigate narrower or shallower passages and stop at smaller ports of call, such as Wrangell and even hard-to-reach Petersburg.

Although Caribbean and Mediterranean cruises have been popular for over half a century, modern cruising to Alaska began in earnest in the mid-1990s, when a handful of companies tentatively launched Inside Passage trips. Now, just a couple of decades later, over 1 million passengers a year – that's over 25 percent more than Alaska's entire population – visit the state with a growing number of cruise operators. Although lots of companies offer a variety of choices, the market is dominated by two mega-players – Princess and Holland America – which compete fiercely for the pre- and post-cruise market by providing their own bus tours, hotels, restaurants, and even luxury domed rail cars, but some passengers prefer more flexible options that can be organized through all cruise companies.

Ruby Princess cruise ship in Alaska

WHERE TO GO

Your first decisions in choosing the cruise that suits you will to be whether you want an Inside Passage only or an Inside Passage plus Gulf of Alaska itinerary; a one-way or a round trip; and a cruise-only or a cruise-plus-extension. Next will be which port of embarkation works best for you. Then, do you want to leave all the logistics to your cruise operator or do you prefer just a cruise with a framework for further nose-following exploration? This guide attempts to introduce and describe the possibilities, along with suggestions and practical information about what to expect from each option.

PORTS OF EMBARKATION

Most of the large cruise ships plying the Alaska routes begin and/or end in Vancouver, British Columbia, Canada. Since the events of 9/11/2001, however, many cruise operators have opted to depart from US ports: mainly Seattle, Washington, or – increasingly – from San Francisco or Los Angeles, California. Because flights are limited to and from Vancouver and all non-Canadians require a passport to visit Canada, these ports also offer easier and more straightforward access, especially for US citizens.

Because one-way cruises are available, many passengers opt to enjoy a land-based vacation in Alaska before or after their cruise. For the southbound trips, the one-way cruises typically begin with a flight to Anchorage, Alaska, then depart from Seward or Whittier, Alaska, and wind up in Vancouver.

Round-trip cruise passengers may also want to consider extensions that take in western North America, especially such attractions as the Canadian Rockies, California, and the US Pacific Northwest.

SEATTLE

There couldn't be a better place to begin any sort of cruise than scenic, water-loving **Seattle**, and an Alaskan cruise will appropriately begin along Alaskan Way, the road that lines Seattle's waterfront. Since almost all of Seattle's many attractions lie within an easy walk or short taxi ride of the cruise terminals, it makes an ideal place to build up to a shipboard adventure or to regain your land legs before heading homeward or launching further travels.

The Waterfront

Before or after a cruise, it's worth strolling along Elliott Bay Trail and inland from the imposing but rather unappealing Alaskan Way viaduct, which is currently an object of contention and is slated for removal and replacement with a tunnel. The area is packed with atmosphere, shopping, and lots of snacking and dining options.

The northern anchor along the **waterfront**, the landmark 520ft (159m) **Space Needle** (Mon–Thu 10am–11pm, Fri–Sat 9am–11.30pm, Sun 9am–11pm; charge; www.spaceneedle. com), serves as Seattle's city icon, and the view from the top provides an overview of the shore, as well as much of the city. Admission can be combined with the adjacent **Chihuly Garden and Glass** (Sun–Thu 11am–8pm, Fri–Sat 11am–9pm; charge; www.chihulygardenandglass.com), featuring the work and collections of the renowned local glass blower, Dale Chihuly. For a more exhilarating overview, including nearby chugging tankers and ferries, ride the 175ft (53m) -high **Seattle Great Wheel** (summer Sun–Thu 10am–11pm, Fri and Sat 10am–midnight;

Pike Place Fish Market, Seattle

charge; www.seattlegreatwheel.com) ferris wheel that is
Seattle's answer to the renowned London Eye.

Another Seattle highlight, **Pike Place Fish Market** (Mon–
Sat 6.30am–6pm, Sun 7am–5pm; www.pikeplacefish.com),
occupies part of the public market beneath the iconic 'Public
Market Center' neon sign. Here, fishmongers ham it up for
tourist cameras, tossing salmon and halibut around and crea-
tively hawking the still slippery merchandise. In the adjacent
market, you'll also find vendors selling cheese, flowers, fruit,
and other delights, and nearby are lots of small shops and
eateries, including what bills itself as the original **Starbuck's**
coffee shop (in fact, it's actually a stone's throw from the site
of the original). Considering that Seattle is almost synonymous
with coffee culture, it could be considered an obligatory stop.

The **Seattle Aquarium** (daily 9.30am–5pm; tel: 206-386
4300; charge; www.seattleaquarium.org), overlooking the

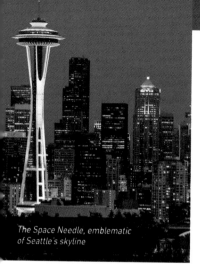
The Space Needle, emblematic of Seattle's skyline

water, features the Window on Washington Waters, an up-close-and-personal view of local sea life. You'll also see captive jellyfish and octopi, but the sea otters, seals, and sea lions steal the show. Try to be there at 11.30am or 2pm for daily talks and feeding.

On a rainy day, it's worth ducking into the **Seattle Art Museum** (Wed and Fri–Sun 10am–5pm, Thu 10am–9pm; charge; www.seatttleartmuseum.org), between Downtown and Pioneer Square. You enter past the animated *Hammering Man* sculpture by Jonathan Borofsky, and inside, you'll find displays of Northwest Native art, Western frontier and romantic paintings, and cutting-edge modern artwork.

Alaska-bound passengers will want to call in at Seattle's portion of the **Klondike Gold Rush National Historical Park** (daily 9am–5pm; tel: 206-220 4240; free; www.nps.gov/klse) – the other half of the park is actually in Skagway, Alaska (see page 73). The rest of the unit includes the beautiful Edwardian and Victorian buildings which surround **Pioneer Square**, a pleasant public space that was once a busy staging area for the Klondike Gold Rush. The park visitors' center is housed in a museum in the 1890 brick-built Cadillac Hotel, which was the digs of choice for hopeful northbound prospectors. The prominent Tlingit totem pole in the center of the square was a 1930s gift to Seattle from the tribe to replace the previous pole, which was smuggled out of Alaska in the late 1800s. The prominent iron pergola dates from the 1909 Alaska-Yukon-Pacific Expo.

Ride the Ducks of Seattle

If the idea of seeing the Seattle sights in a WWII amphibious vehicle with a slapstick guide appeals, then hop on the popular **Ride the Ducks of Seattle Tour** (tel: 206-441 3825; www. ridetheducksofseattle.com). The tour covers the route between Pioneer Square and Lake Union (including an amphibious lake crossing), stopping along the way at Pike Place Fish Market, the Space Needle, and such 'unmissable' icons as the flagship Starbucks coffee shop and the first Nordstrom store, which once sold only shoes.

Tillicum Village

The popular half-day excursion to **Tillicum Village** with Argosy Cruises (Pier 55, 1101 Alaskan Way; tel: 206-623 1445; www. argosycruises.com) begins with a small-boat cruise from Pier 55 to Blake Island State Park. There, you'll enjoy a quintessential Pacific Northwest buffet, including fresh alder-roasted fish, followed by a Northwest Native tribes story-telling production. The same company also runs convenient cruises around Lake Union and Lake Washington.

Mt Rainier

The looming 14,410ft (4,400m) high volcano, Mt Rainier, dominates the Seattle backdrop and forms the centerpiece of the incredibly beautiful **Mt Rainier National Park** (tel: 360-569 2211; charge; www.nps.gov/mora), which is full of wondrous forests, streams, waterfalls, and excellent drives and hiking trails, as well as the great peak itself. At 80 miles (128km) from

Seattle, it makes an ideal day excursion for nature lovers; for ideas, see www.visitrainier.com.

VANCOUVER

Lying between the Coast Range mountains and the sea, **Vancouver**, British Columbia, Canada's quintessentially cosmopolitan Pacific port, is habitually voted as one of the world's most liveable cities. That makes it an attraction in itself, as well as an excellent launch point for an Alaska cruise. Cruises arrive and depart at the Canada Place Cruise Ship Terminal (999 Canada Place, Vancouver, BC V6C 3E1; tel: 604-665 9000; www.portvancouver.com/cruise), which is right in downtown Vancouver.

Downtown

Canada Place and its Trade and Convention Center, built as the Canada pavilion for Expo 86 and used as a media center for the 2010 Winter Olympics, is meant to approximate a cruise ship leaving port and similarities to the Sydney Opera House are apparent. The sails house the main cruise ship terminal for Alaska cruises, so this is where you'll arrive or depart. Happily, it's within an easy walk, ferry ride, or Skytrain trip from numerous sites of interest.

Hugely popular with kids is **Telus World of Science** (late Jun–early Sep Sun–Wed 10am–6pm, Thu 10am–10pm, Fri–Sat 10am–8pm; charge; www.scienceworld.ca) at the waterfront Expo 86 site. The dome has more than 350 interactive displays. Attached to the site is the **OMNIMAX Theatre**, the largest screen of its kind in the world.

The enigmatic **Gastown** neighbourhood, named for the early pub owner 'Gassy' Jack Deighton, makes an ideal place to stroll and explore near the cruise dock. With cobbled streets and gas

streetlamps, an undeni-
ably bohemian atmosphere
overlies lots of tourist-
oriented shops, galleries,
cafés, and restaurants.

On the corner of Robson
and Howe streets is the
Vancouver Art Gallery
(Wed–Mon 10am–5pm, Tue
10am–9pm; charge; www.
vanartgallery.bc.ca), with
its impressive collection
of works by both Canadian
and international artists.

Gastown's working
Steam Clock, one of
only a few in the world

The **Granville Island
Public Market** (open
daily) began as an experiment in the late 1970s to turn a
collection of abandoned buildings and heavy industries
into a place to buy fresh produce. Here you'll find everything from artisanal chocolates to wild mushrooms and
seaweeds, with an emphasis on locally grown and created
products. There are restaurants and bars, as well as two
brewing companies and even a sake maker. Another urban
food mecca is **Chinatown**, just east of the downtown core,
but a world apart.

Between the university and downtown is the **Museum of
Vancouver** (Sun–Wed 10am–5pm, Thu 10am–8pm, Fri–Sat
10am–9pm; charge; www.museumofvancouver.ca), tracing the
city's history from the First Nations settlement to the arrival of
Europeans and the modern city. On the same grounds, the **H.R.
MacMillan Space Centre** (mid-Jul–early Sep daily 10am–5pm,
observatory 8pm–midnight, evening astronomy shows 7.30pm

and 9pm; charge; www.spacecentre.ca), features a planetarium, observatory, motion simulator, and theater.

The nearby **Vancouver Maritime Museum** (Mon–Wed and Fri–Sat 10am–5pm, Thu 10am–8pm, Sun noon–5pm; charge; www.vancouvermaritimemuseum.com), preserves the RCMP schooner, the *St Roch,* which made two trips through the Northwest Passage and established Canada's supremacy over its Arctic region. Nearby, at **Heritage Harbor**, historic ships are moored during summer.

Stanley Park

The 1,000-acre (405-hectare) thumb of forest known as **Stanley Park** juts into Burrard Inlet and provides a green oasis of Douglas fir, cedar, and hemlock. It was dedicated in 1889 in the name of governor general, Lord Stanley, who also gave his name to professional hockey's grand prize, the Stanley Cup. The park's prominent 10km (6-mile) perimeter sea wall offers a panoramic view of the city skyline and the intervening water, with its many passing watercraft, from kayak to cargo ship. The park also boasts a collection of nine **totem poles** from the Kwakwaka'wakw, Haida, and Squamish First Nations. Another park

Totem pole in Stanley Park

highlight is the **Vancouver Aquarium** (late Jun to early Sep daily 9.30am–6pm, May–late Jun daily 10am–5pm; charge; www.vanaqua.org), with 70,000 residents that include dolphins and beluga whales.

University Area

On the campus of the University of British Columbia, the **Museum of Anthropology** (mid-May–mid-Oct daily 10am–5pm; charge; www.moa.ubc.ca) contains an outstanding collection of totem poles, including a full-size replica of a West Coast native village complete with longhouses. Also at the UBC campus, the **Nitobe Memorial Garden** (mid-Mar–Oct daily 11am–4.30pm; charge; tours available; www.botanicalgarden.ubc.ca) is considered among the top five traditional Japanese gardens outside Japan, featuring cherry blossoms in spring, irises in summer and brilliant maple hues in autumn. The university-affiliated **Greenheart TreeWalk** (daily Apr–Oct; charge) is a 1,010ft- (308m-) aerial trail system where visitors traverse bridges suspended in 100-year-old trees. The trails are 50–65ft (15–20m) above the ground, with several viewing platforms joining the walkways. Admission is combined with a ticket to Nitobe Memorial Garden.

Victoria

British Columbia's British-tinted capital, the historic trading port of Victoria, at the southern tip of Vancouver Island, is a port of call for some cruises starting in Seattle, San Francisco, and Los Angeles. Ships dock at Ogden Point, a mile from downtown, with shuttle services available. A requisite shore excursion would be a city tour including lovely **Butchart Gardens** (daily 8.45am–10pm; www.butchartgardens.com) at Brentwood Bay, 13 miles (21km) from Victoria, where visitors can take high tea among the English, Japanese, and Continental-themed gardens.

Whistler

The internationally renowned **Whistler Village Ski Resort,** an excellent shore excursion 62 miles (100km) north of Vancouver, evolved from a gondola and a few T-bars serving local skiers to one of the top North American ski resorts and a venue in the 2010 Winter Olympics. This is partly due to its year-round activities and careful emulation of a European village, but the real reason is the two spectacular mountains, Whistler and Blackcomb, which are linked by the Peak 2 Peak Gondola, the longest (2 miles/3.2km) and highest (1,430ft/436m) cable car span in the world. In summer, golf, mountain biking, and hiking trails attract visitors for the day or for much longer. Exceptional food and drink reward a day of hiking, skiing, or braving the zipline – a series of 10 individual steel cables strung across 8,100ft (2,470m) of forest, interspersed with suspension bridges and viewing platforms.

⊘ BC FERRIES & SMALL BRITISH COLUMBIA PORTS

The provincial BC Ferries (tel: 250-386 3431, www.bcferries.com) runs scheduled services along the rugged British Columbia Inside Passage between Vancouver (Horseshoe Bay or Tsawwassen), Nanaimo, and Victoria (Swartz Bay), and between Port Hardy (on Vancouver Island five hours' by road north of Nanaimo) and Bella Bella, Klemtu, and the logging and lumbering port of Prince Rupert at the terminus of Canada's Yellowhead Highway (where BC Ferries connect with the Alaska Marine Highway). Some small cruise lines and charter operators, as well as the innovative Seabourn Cruiselines, also call in at these places, and some even feature the wild and rain-battered Haida Gwaii (Queen Charlotte) islands.

SAN FRANCISCO

Historically, **San Francisco** served as a jumping-off point for the 49er prospectors heading for the California gold rush, making it analagous to Seattle during the Klondike and Alaska gold rushes. Today, thanks to Oceania and Princess Cruises, it is rapidly joining Seattle as a popular US jumping-off point for Alaska cruising. Most cruises berth at the James R Herman cruise

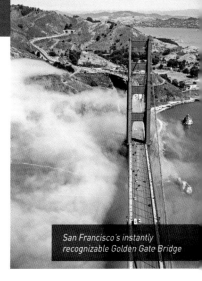

San Francisco's instantly recognizable Golden Gate Bridge

terminal (tel: 415-274 0400; www.sfport.com) at Pier 27 on the Embarcadero – on the San Francisco Bay side of the peninsula, with an excellent view of the four-masted Bay Bridge. When more than one cruise ship is in port, they also use the nearby Pier 35.

San Francisco is undoubtedly one of the most beautiful, vibrant, and diverse cities in the US, if not the world. Sitting at the end of a 32-mile (50km) peninsula, this city of seven hills is surrounded by water on three sides and blessed by one of the world's great natural harbors, making it an ideal port city.

The peninsula is joined to the main body of California by two masterpieces of bridge design, including the unmistakeable **Golden Gate Bridge**, which is often obscured by a blanket of fog. Beyond the iconic sites – the grand bridges, rattling cable cars, and barking sea lions – there are over a dozen distinct and wonderfully original neighborhoods to explore, each with its own appeal. And whether it's innovative cuisine, fine art,

The Coit Tower and island-prison of Alcatraz

classical music, contemporary dance, sprawling parks, or boisterous street festivals you're after, you will be sure to find it in the wonderful 'city by the bay'.

Fisherman's Wharf Area

Within strolling distance of the cruise ship dock at pier 27 is the rather touristy **Fisherman's Wharf.** This bright, family-oriented carnival of attractions, despite the crowds and occasional tackiness, is full of seafood restaurants, small stores tucked between the souvenir stands, and narrow boardwalks jammed with sightseers. With all the opportunities for exploring, shopping, people-watching, and fine seafood dining, it's easy to forget that much of San Francisco's maritime past is moored in this historic district.

The waterfront retrospective starts at the **Hyde Street Pier**, where a fleet of vintage vessels is docked, including a sidewheel ferry and three schooners that carried heavy freight in the days of sailing ships. The tall masts and rigging at the water's edge belong to the graceful Scottish-built Balclutha, a 301ft (92m) clipper built in 1886 that made 17 trips around Cape Horn. These ships belong to the adjacent **Maritime Museum** (daily 10am–4pm; tel: 415-561 7100; free; www.nps.gov/safr), part of the San Francisco Maritime National Historical Park, which displays intricate models of boats and muralist Hilaire Hiler's surrealist vision of the Atlantis. It is located in **Aquatic Park**, a terraced green that leads out to a small beach and curving municipal fishing pier. South of the Maritime Museum, the Civil War-era woolens mill turned chocolate factory, **Ghirardelli Square**, is now a trendy and popular shopping center geared towards visitors, and the chocolate probably shouldn't be missed.

Telegraph Hill

Prominent **Telegraph Hill** is crowned by the 210ft (64m) **Coit Tower** (summer 10am–5.30pm; tel: 415-362 0808; charge to take elevator), which is shaped like a fire hose in honor of city firefighters. Built in 1934 on the site of an early telegraph station and funded by heiress Lillie Hitchcock Coit, it lures visitors with a series of city life murals and momentous 360-degree views over city and sea. Down its eastern slope are the lovely Filbert and Greenwich street staircases, flanked by attractive and lush private gardens that are home to the flock of wild red-headed parrots who starred in the 2003 documentary *The Wild Parrots of Telegraph Hill*.

Chinatown

Chinatown, San Francisco's 24-block Asian enclave is a remnant of the Gold Rush days, when Chinese workers were imported in large numbers to build the trans-continental railroads. It's entered through the green pagoda-topped **Chinatown Gate** at the corner of Bush Street and Grant Avenue, which was gifted by China in 1969. Through the gate, dragon-topped lampposts and crisscrossing lines of red lanterns run the length of **Grant Avenue**, Chinatown's main tourist street, and shop windows beckon with crowded displays of

San Fran's iconic cable cars

silk, porcelain, hand-painted vases, teak furniture, and lots of less-appealing souvenirs. Food ranges from tiny cafés and obscure eateries to popular dim sum lunch spots. It's on the narrow streets intersecting Grant that Chinatown becomes an enigmatic place to explore.

Mission Dolores

The renowned Mission District takes its name from **Mission Dolores** (summer daily 9am–5pm; tel: 415-621 8203; charge; www.missiondolores.org), the sixth mission in the chain of 21 Spanish settlements that stretched 650 miles (1,050km) from San Diego to Sonoma, north of San Francisco. Mission Dolores was founded less than a week before the American Declaration of Independence was signed in 1776, and its thick adobe walls still form what is the oldest building in San Francisco.

Cable Cars

Even from their earliest days, San Francisco's famous **cable cars** (www.sfcablecar.com) impressed visitors. Operating on three routes – the Powell–Mason, Powell–Hyde and California lines – San Francisco's cable cars are among the last in the United States, at least 100 cities having abandoned them for buses. The most enjoyable routes for visitors are the Powell–Mason and Powell–Hyde lines, which share a terminus at Powell and Market and then diverge in Nob Hill on different routes to Fisherman's Wharf. Powell–Hyde is the more scenic, passing through Russian Hill and the top of twisting Lombard Street.

Alcatraz

Just over a mile offshore and accessible only by ferry, **Alcatraz** (daily tours from Pier 33; tel: 415-981 7625; charge; www.alcatraz cruises.com and www.nps.gov/altcatraz.com) attracts visitors with tales of legendary inmates from the Prohibition and Mafia heyday. Sighted in 1775 by Spanish Lieutenant Juan Manuel de Ayala, this tiny lump of rock appeared to be inhabited only by pelicans, and – not surprisingly – Ayala named it Isla de los Alcatraces, or the Island of Pelicans. It was first used as a military garrison in the 1850s, but because escape from the island would require a near impossible swim through frigid waters and swift currents, it became a prison for servicemen, renegade Indians, and Spanish-American War prisoners.

Alcatraz eventually evolved into the notorious federal prison of its current reputation, holding such legendary characters as Mafia don Al Capone and the gangster bootlegger Machine Gun Kelly. The few desperate inmates who attempted escape invariably perished in the cold waters. The prison was finally closed in 1963 when repairs grew too costly. The site is now managed by the US National Park Service as part of the Golden

Astoria, Oregon

Perhaps best-known as the place where in 1805 the Lewis and Clark expedition reached the Pacific Ocean, the enigmatic port of Astoria, Oregon, at the mouth of the mighty Columbia River, makes a convenient port of call for Alaska-bound ships setting out from Los Angeles or San Francisco. Currently, the major player here is Oceania Cruises, whose shore excursions include an ale tour, a wine tour, and longer excursions to Lewis and Clark sites, Mt St Helens, and the dramatic Oregon Coast.

Gate National Recreation Area. Ranger-guided tours include a peek at some of the cell blocks, and an evocative, award-winning taped tour features audio of some of the early prisoners.

LOS ANGELES

A sprawling city of 18 million, **Los Angeles** may be the United States' second largest city, but it's perhaps best described as a vast metropolis suffering from schizophrenic tendencies – and its various personalities may not always interact well. Nevertheless, forward-looking from the start, Los Angeles has been a mecca for the young and hopeful since the 1950s, and it is still a magnet for those seeking a new life, or – most of all – to join the ranks of the stars (or at least see one in his or her own habitat).

Alaska cruises to and from Los Angeles operate from the World Cruise Center (100 Swinford Street, San Pedro, CA 90731; tel: 310-519 2342; www.portoflosangeles.org), or the Carnival Cruise Port (231 Windsor Way, Long Beach, CA 90802; tel: 562-901 3232; http://tinyurl.com/2d5fna). There's little of interest within walking distance of either, so exploration will require using a taxi, working out the sparse and time-consuming bus system, or renting a car.

Downtown

In **Downtown LA**, millions of dollars have been spent to bring in modern architecture, cultural institutions, and high-end lofts, now interspersed among the ornate movie palaces and other unforgettable fixtures from the past. The restored historic **City Hall** (observation deck Mon–Fri 8am–5pm) was built using sand from every California county and water from every historic Spanish mission. The grand **Walt Disney Concert Hall** (daily 10am–2pm; tel: 323-850 2000; free tours most days; www.laphil.com), with striking stainless steel curves, an enormous pipe organ, and Douglas fir panels, is home to the LA Philharmonic. A block further along Grand Avenue is the **Museum of Contemporary Art (MOCA)** (Mon, Wed and Fri 11am–6pm, Thu 11am–8pm, Sat–Sun 11am–5pm; tel: 213-626

City Hall, Downtown LA

Grauman's Chinese Theatre in Hollywood

6222; charge; www.moca.org), which features American and European art from the 1940s to the present. When you need a snack, head for lively **Olvera Street** (www.olvera-street.com) to enjoy the most authentic Mexican street food to be found north of the border.

Hollywood

Hollywood, as almost everyone knows, is a Los Angeles icon. Start at **Grauman's Chinese Theatre** (charge; www.tclchinesetheatres.com), the famous landmark most notable for its forecourt of famous footprints. Nearby are the neo-Gothic **Hollywood First National Bank Building**, at the corner of Highland Avenue, and, east of La Brea, the glamorous **Hollywood Roosevelt Hotel**, site of the first public Oscars ceremony in 1929. **The Kodak Theatre**, where the Oscars ceremony is staged, is part of the shop- and restaurant-filled **Hollywood and Highland Center** (tel: 323-308 6363; charge for tours; www.kodaktheatre.com). In a 30-minute guided tour, visitors have access to VIP areas and the low-down on the gossip and glitz of the event. The old Max Factor building on Highland just south of Hollywood is now the **Hollywood Museum** (Wed–Sun 10am–5pm; tel: 323-464 7776; charge), which displays costumes, film posters, and artifacts, including Cary Grant's Rolls-Royce. Across the street is the approach to the **Hollywood Bowl** (www.hollywoodbowl.com), an 18,000-seat amphitheater staging classical music, jazz, world music, and major rock performances.

The **Hollywood Walk of Fame** (www.walkoffame.com) is the area today that most visitors think of as the heart of Hollywood: the celebrated brass and terrazzo stars along it run along Hollywood Boulevard westwards from Vine Street, with Marilyn Monroe's star outside the McDonald's restaurant.

La Brea

The **La Brea Tar Pits** at the Page Museum (daily 10am–5pm; tel: 323-934 7243; charge) was once the source of asphalt used to pave the streets of San Francisco, but in 1889, the company geologists began uncovering millions of fossilized bones of saber-toothed tigers, giant sloths and extinct wolves that had become trapped in the tar, but the only human remains found there was the skeleton of a woman who lived 9,000 years earlier.

Beverly Hills

With the rise of Hollywood, filmdom's elite built ever-bigger homes in elegant **Beverly Hills**, which fans out into the hills and canyons, and around spectacular **Mulholland Drive**, which runs for 50 miles (80km) along the crest of the Santa Monica Mountains to the coast north of Malibu. Here, and in adjacent **Laurel Canyon**, the Hollywood rich and famous, as well as a host of 1960s rock stars, established lavish homes where they luxuriated in their ample wealth.

Along famous **Rodeo Drive** between Santa Monica and Wilshire boulevards are packed designer stores with such familiar names as Gucci, Hermès, Chanel, Fendi, and Cartier. At the rather whimsical Two Rodeo Drive, with its cobbled street and bow windows, is a replica of what only Hollywood could believe to be an olde-worlde European backwater.

The Coast

Head west on Pacific Coast Highway (PCH) to reach the wealthy seaside community of **Malibu**, with its free state beach and pier. Around the lagoon, you can spot ducks, herons, and pelicans, and not far away lies the star-studded but well-guarded Malibu Colony. The Malibu coastline is private but only down to the mean high-tide line – meaning that as long as you stay on wet sand, you have every right to be there.

Santa Monica is the largest coastal suburb on the 100-mile (160-km) stretch between Oxnard and Long Beach, and it has attracted residents from the media and the arts. The century-old **Santa Monica Pier** has numerous amusement arcades, a carousel (used in *The Sting* and *Forest Gump*), and eating places and fishing stands from which visitors have gorgeous views of Pacific sunsets and curving beaches.

Then there's Venice. An early favorite of such silent movie-makers as Charlie Chaplin and Carole Lombard, **Venice Boardwalk** is today jammed almost around the clock with characters who provide evidence that in Los Angeles, the outrageous and otherwise abnormal can seem rather mundane.

For a cultural injection, check out the imposing **Getty Center** (Tue–Thu and Sun 10am–5.30pm, Fri–Sat 10am–9pm; tel: 310-440 7300; free, but charge for parking; www.getty.edu). Overlooking Santa Monica, it has been likened to a Tuscan hilltown by its award-winning architect, Richard Meier, who was chosen for the commission after a worldwide search. He described the site as 'the most beautiful I have ever been invited to build upon'. The museum, which occupies five interconnecting buildings, features European drawings, paintings and sculpture, French 17th- and 18th-century decorative arts, and photography.

Disneyland

There's nothing quite like the original **Disneyland** (hours vary; 1313 Harbor Boulevard, Anaheim; tel: 714-781 4000; charge; www.disneyland.disney.go.com), first opened with the tagline "Magic Kingdom" in 1955. There's no way to avoid the crowds, especially in summer, but to see as much of the park as possible, cover it one "land" at a time: Fantasyland, Adventureland, Frontierland, Critter Country, and jazzy New Orleans Square.

SOUTHERN PANHANDLE

The gateway to Alaska for northbound cruises, the **Southern Panhandle** is home to a handful of idyllic, often rain-drenched towns and villages that open onto pristine waterways and are

Ship docked at Ketchikan, the gateway to northbound cruises to Alaska

backed up against soaring, heavily forested peaks. Road access to the region is limited to tiny Hyder, at the end of Portland Canal, but none of the cruise ship or ferry ports of call are connected to the North American highway system.

KETCHIKAN

The 'First City' of **Ketchikan** ❶, Alaska's first port of call for northbound cruises, tumbles down the densely forested, mountainous, southwestern side of Revillagigedo Island, where stacks of steep-roofed houses cling to the thickly forested slopes while the business district spills over onto pilings in Tongass Narrows.

Ketchikan likes to call itself the 'Salmon Capital of the World' and many the area's 14,000 residents do work in commercial fishing and fish processing, while the most of the rest are occupied in tourism and logging.

Downtown and Dock Area

The Ketchikan cruise docks lie within walking distance of several attractions. The **Ketchikan Visitors Bureau** Ⓐ (Mon–Fri 8am–5pm, Sat–Sun 6am–6pm; tel: 907-225 6166; www.visit-ketchikan.com), at Berth 2 of the cruise ship dock, hands out walking tour maps and other information.

The nearest must-see is **Creek Street** Ⓑ (www.creekstreet ketchikan.com), the historic red-light district where in times past, 'both the fishermen and the fish went upstream to spawn'. Here a rustic-looking wooden walkway above Ketchikan Creek leads through a colorful array of gift shops, galleries, restaurants, coffee shops, and **Dolly's House** Ⓒ (May–Oct daily 8am–5pm; tel: 907-225 6329; charge; http://dollyshouse.com), a popular brothel-turned-museum. Along the way, a **funicular tram** Ⓓ travels up the steep mountainside to Cape Fox Lodge, which affords a great view over the town. Eventually, the boardwalk gives way to the whimsically-named 'Married Man's Trail' – the sneaky back entrance to Creek Street.

The **Southeast Alaska Discovery Center** Ⓔ (May–Sep daily 8am–4pm; tel: 907-228 6220; free; www.alaskacenters.gov/ketchikan.cfm) provides an overview of the Tongass, the temperate rainforest that covers most of Southeast Alaska and makes up the largest National Forest in the US. The center also displays authentic totems, Native artists in residence, cultural exhibits, and a gift shop.

Another popular shore activity is the light-hearted and engaging **Great Alaskan Lumberjack Show** Ⓕ (May–Sep four shows daily; tel: 907-225 9050; charge; http://alaskanlumberjackshow.com), where teams of husky lumberjacks entertain spectators

Shops have replaced brothels on Creek Street

Ziplining is an exhilarating way to see the rainforest

with their Bunyanesque antics.

If you're short on time and can't make it to Saxman or Totem Bight State Historical Park (see below) to see the totem poles, examples from all three local tribes – the Tlingit, Haida and Tsimshian – are displayed just a short taxi ride from the cruise ship dock at the **Totem Heritage Center** (601 Deermount Street; May–Sep daily 8am–5pm; tel: 907-225 5900; www.ktn-ak.us/totem-heritage-center).

Alaska Canopy Ziplining

Ziplining from one tree top platform to the next offers a unique way to see the temperate rainforest, particularly when the course includes gliding over waterfalls and salmon spawning streams. These ideal shore excursions, which must be pre-booked, take three to four hours. For details, contact Alaska Canopy Adventures (tel: 907-225 5503; www.alaskacanopy.com).

Totem Bight State Historical Park

Totem Bight State Historical Park ❷ (daily 7.30am–around 6pm; tel: 907-225-4445; charge; dnr.alaska.gov/parks/units/totembgh.htm), 10 miles (16km) north of the city center, occupies a beautiful wooded area facing the Tongass Narrows on the site of an ancient Tlingit fishing ground. This state park features 12 full-sized totem poles, five intricately carved tribal houses, a busy carving center, museums featuring antique cars and firearms, Native art displays, and a gift shop.

Saxman Totem Park

An alternative for seeing totem poles is the **Saxman Totem Park** ❸ in the Native village of Saxman, 2 miles (3km) south of Ketchikan, which is actually an incorporated city of 410 – mostly Tlingit – residents. The Cape Fox Corporation (www. capefoxtours.com) offers a **Saxman Native Village Tour**, featuring a beautiful tribal house complete with an iconic 'frog wall' and lots of totem poles, an active carving center, and a presentation by the Cape Fox Dance group.

Misty Fiords National Monument

The 3,570 sq-mile (9,240 sq km) **Misty Fjords National Monument** ❹, 40 miles (64km) south of Ketchikan, is a magical place, carved out by the steady progress of gigantic glaciers, colored by pristine forests and towering waterfalls, and animated

---

⊘ THE TEMPERATE RAINFOREST

The world's largest temperate rainforest covers much of the coastal US Pacific Northwest and almost all of Canada's Pacific coast, plus all non-glacial areas of Southeast Alaska, and is both a natural resource and a beautiful emerald backdrop for the entire Inside Passage. Receiving 60 to 100 inches (150–250cm) of rain annually, it's characterized by a rain-soaked forest floor of lush lichens, mosses, and ferns beneath a canopy of conifers: Sitka spruce, western hemlock, mountain hemlock, yellow cedar, western red cedar, silver fir, and Pacific yew.

Floatplane flying over the Misty Fjords National Monument

by abundant wildlife. Within its largely untouched coast and backcountry lie three major rivers, hundreds of small streams and creeks, icefields, glaciers, old-growth rainforest, snow-capped mountains, and mountain-top lakes.

A monument highlight is the volcanic 'plug' rising from the water known as New Eddystone Rock. It was named by the British navigator Captain George Vancouver (1758–98) – after whom the Canadian city is named – because he thought it resembled Eddystone Lighthouse off the shore of his hometown of Plymouth, England.

The monument is accessed by boat or floatplane and in the summer, tours often coincide with ship schedules. Some travelers opt for a combination cruise/fly tour – going in by water and out by air, or vice versa. You can fly there with a Ketchikan air charter company, cruise there by charter boat such as Alaska Coastal Quest (2729 Tongass Ave; tel: 907-225 3498), or flight-see with local air taxi Taquan Air (4085 Tongass Ave; tel: 907-225 8800; www.taquanair.com).

METLAKATLA

The small Tsimshian village of **Metlakatla** ❺, in Alaska's only Indian Reservation, sits on Annette Island about 15 miles (25km) south of Ketchikan. Served only by the Alaska Marine

Highway and Windstar Cruises – and therefore, still well off the beaten track – this charming and tidy little place was founded in 1887 when Anglican missionary Father William Duncan and 823 parishioners migrated from British Columbia after they fell out with the church in Canada. Today, the town features a picturesque cannery on stilts over the harbor, plus the **Duncan Cottage Museum** (tel: 907-886-3637; https://wdcmuseum. weebly.com), a **Tsimshian clan house**, and a scattered collection of totem poles.

WRANGELL

The heavily forested island community of **Wrangell** ⑥, 89 miles (143km) north of Ketchikan, is a laid-back, working town of about 2,800 residents, many of whom, for generations, have logged the Tongass, worked in local sawmills, or fished commercially. Due to the narrow channels surrounding the island, Wrangell is not a stop for the larger cruise ships, but the community welcomes smaller ships with an ambience less affected by tourism than more popular ports of call.

Downtown and Dock Area

There are many sights unique to this delightful and compact town. On your

Totem Poles

Contrary to popular belief, the totem poles of Alaska's Tlingit, Haida, and Tsimshian peoples were never meant to be venerated. Instead, they served as recognition of specific clan affiliations – Raven, Wolf, Frog, Bear, Whale, etc – or to commemorate events or tell stories. Early Christian missionaries misunderstood and discouraged their use, but today, old poles are being renovated, master carvers are creating new ones, and the craft is being passed along to young apprentices.

Coastal brown bear hunting for salmon

way past the **city dock**, young merchants sell garnets dug from Wrangell's **Garnet Ledge** (www.wrangellgarnetledge.com). For information, drop by the **Wrangell Convention & Visitors Bureau** (296 Campbell Drive; tel: 800-367 9745; www.wrangellalaska.org), which also houses the **Wrangell Museum** (May–Sep Mon–Sat 10am–5pm; tel: 907-874 3770), with exhibits on the town's gold mining, timber, fishing, and trapping history. The visitor center's staff will connect you with tour operators who can arrange excursions on foot or by helicopter, kayak, boat, bus, or plane.

Take a stroll out to **Chief Shakes Island**, accessible year-round by a walkway into Wrangell harbor, with its intricately carved Tlingit totems and **Chief Shakes Tribal House** (by appointment only; tel: 907-874 4304; http://shakesisland.com).

Also worthwhile is **Petroglyph Beach ❼** (1 mile/1.6km from the dock), a State Historic Park with a collection of at least 40 ancient rock carvings whose origins remain a mystery. After photographing the petroglyphs, you can use the replicas on the observation deck to make rubbings.

Out of Town

Just a mile (1.6km) north of town, Wrangell attempts to emulate balmier ports of call with its USGA-rated, nine-hole golf course, **Muskeg Meadows** ❽ (tel: 907-874 4653; www. wrangellalaskagolf.com).

A 28-mile (45km) boat trip up the Stikine River will land you at the collection of open-air hot tubs known as **Chief Shakes Hot Springs** ❾, where you can enjoy a soothing hot tub experience and also soak up a bit of real wilderness magic. Bring a swim suit and bottled water.

A boat or floatplane ride to the **Anan Creek Bear and Wildlife Observatory** ❿ (Jul–Aug 8am–6pm; tel: 907-874 2323), 30 miles (48km) southeast of Wrangell, provides an opportunity to see brown and black bears, plus bald eagles and sea lions, feasting on one of Southeast Alaska's largest pink salmon runs. Bears are viewed from a covered platform overlooking a

---

⊙ ALASKA'S BEARS

Alaska is Bear Country, USA, and unless you're in the Aleutian Islands, you're never far from a bear here. Brown bears (*Ursus arctos*) range from Southeast Alaska to the Arctic slope. On the coast, they grow to enormous size – up to 1,000lbs (540kg) – due to their fish diet. The smaller grizzly bears are the same species, but they live inland and don't grow as big because they eat less protein. Black bears (*Ursus americanus*) inhabit roughly the same territory, but keep mainly to forested areas. They're also smaller and range in color from black and cinnamon to blue and almost white (the white variant, called the 'spirit bear', is endemic mainly along the northern British Columbia coast). The enormous white polar bears (*Ursus maritimus*), the largest of the three species, live along the Arctic Ocean coast and can weigh over 1,500lbs (680kg).

waterfall. In peak season, permits are essential (tel: 877-444 6777; www.recreation.gov).

PETERSBURG

The picturesque fishing town of **Petersburg** ⑪, on the north-west end of Mitkof Island, likes to call itself 'Little Norway', in honor of the heritage of most of its 3,100 residents. Large cruise ships can't navigate the cramped Wrangell Narrows to reach it, but those aboard an increasing number of smaller cruise ships calling in there can avail themselves to its scenic, small-town charms.

Downtown and Dock Area

The **Visitor Information Center** (summer Mon–Sat 9am–5pm, Sun noon–4pm; tel: 907-772 4636; www.petersburg.org) will help you pack your stop with activities, including guided boat, floatplane, helicopter, kayak, glacier-viewing, whale-watching, and fishing tours.

Most attractions lie within easy walking distance and the town, known for its scenic surroundings and unique public art displays, is an attraction in itself. Be sure to see the interesting concrete stamps along the sidewalks and the colorful *rosemaling* (Norwegian tole painting) on many homes and storefronts. You'll also see a variety of murals, totems, and sculptures by local artisans on public display.

The **Sing Lee Alley** boardwalk, on pilings along **Hammer Slough,** where the creek empties into the harbor area, is lined with photogenic weathered shops and boathouses. The **Sons of Norway Hall** (www.petersburgsons.org), with the Viking ship *Valhalla* sitting out front, offers summer visitors a buffet of Norwegian pastries, fish cakes, and pickled herring (times coincide with cruise-ship arrivals).

The small but tasteful **Clausen Memorial Museum** (May–Sep Mon–Sat 10am–5pm; tel: 907-772 3598; http://clausenmuseum.com) tells Petersburg's undeniably fishy story from both the Tlingit and Norwegian perspective.

Eagle Roost Park (www.petersburgrec.com), a short stroll away along North Nordic Drive, provides a platform for viewing roosting bald eagles, as well as a pathway to the beach to explore the lovely tide pools.

Houses on stilts, Petersburg

KAKE

A few small ships, as well as the Alaska Marine Highway, call in at the tiny Tlingit village of **Kake** ⑫, on well-logged Kupreanof Island. Lauded as perhaps the next Icy Strait Point (that is, a ready-made cruise port), Kake remains small, friendly, and relatively undeveloped. Situated on Frederick Sound, it's an excellent spot for whale-watching, and the town itself boasts a **historic old cannery** and a 128ft (39m) totem pole – one of the world's largest – which was carved in 1967 for the centennial of Alaska's purchase from Russia.

SITKA

Sitka ⑬, on the west coast of Baranof Island, is a showcase of Alaska's unique and complex mix of Native, Russian, and

American cultures and the only Southeast Alaskan port directly facing the Pacific Ocean.

When the first Russian explorer Vitus Bering arrived in 1741, this wild land was occupied by the Tlingit, who had a trading culture that extended down the Pacific coast as far as the Seattle area. Fifty years later, Alexander Baranov, of the Russian-American Company, built a fort and trading post, St Michael's Redoubt, just north of the present town.

Fearing Russian domination and enslavement, the Tlingit attacked the redoubt in 1802, killing most of the settlers, but two years later, Baranov retaliated by bringing a Russian warship to bombard the village. The Tlingit fought bravely for six days in what came to be known as the Battle of Sitka, but were eventually driven from the area. The Russians then re-established the settlement and renamed it 'New Archangel.' Sitka was designated the capital of Russian America, and after Alaska was transferred to the US in 1867, it became the territorial capital, a title it held until 1906, when the capital was moved to Juneau.

As a port of call, Sitka isn't yet as popular as Ketchikan or Juneau, but more cruise lines are adding it to their itineraries due to the many worthwhile things to see and do within easy walking distance of the harbor.

Totem pole in the Sitka National Historical Park

Downtown and Dock Area

The city's narrow streets, all convenient to the dock, are dotted with beautifully restored historic buildings, making them inviting for a stroll around the sights. A convenient first stop is the **Harrigan Centennial Hall,** which houses the **Visitors Center** (330 Harbor Drive; tel: 907-747 3225; www.cityof sitka.com/government/departments/centennial). Here you'll find contacts for various tour operators who run guided tours around town by semi-submersible vessel, all-terrain vehicle (ATV), bike, bus, or on foot. They also post schedules for performances of Russian folk songs and dances by the **New Archangel Dancers** (tel: 907-747 5516; www.new-archangeldancers.com), an amateur troupe formed in 1969 to preserve Sitka's Russian heritage through dance.

The **Alaska Raptor Center** (1000 Raptor Way; May–Sep daily 8am–4pm; tel: 907-747 8662 or 800-643 9425; charge; www. alaskaraptor.org) provides medical treatment for injured bald eagles (and other birds), and conducts bald eagle research. Visitors have an opportunity for close-up raptor observation.

A short stroll over the Indian River and through old-growth rainforest lies the visitors' center of the beautiful **Sitka National Historical Park ⓮** (May–Sep daily 8am–5pm; tel: 907-747 0110; www.nps.gov/sitk). A network of trails winds through the 100-acre (40-hectare) park, lined with colorful Tlingit totem poles, the remains of historic Tlingit and Russian structures, and the 1804 battleground. The visitors' center museum displays exhibits on Native American history and art. Ranger-guided tours are conducted daily in the summer.

A short walk away is the **Sheldon Jackson Museum** (mid-May–Sep daily 9am–5pm; tel: 907-747 8981; charge; www. museums.state.ak.us/sheldon_jackson/sjhome.html), Alaska's oldest museum, which features an extensive collection of

Native artifacts that were gathered between 1888 and 1898. At the **Sitka Sound Science Center** (May–Sep Mon–Sat 9am–4pm; tel: 907-747 8878; donation requested; www.sitkascience. org), you can visit an aquarium with touch tanks and a hatchery, and next door, enjoy a bowl of delicious local clam chowder at Ludvig's Chowder Cart (www.ludvigsbistro.com).

The **Russian Bishop's House** (103 Monastery Street; daily May–Sep 9am–5pm; tel: 907-747 0110; free; www.nps.gov/ sitk), built in 1842, is an excellent example of restored Russian colonial architecture, complete with original furniture, appliances, and articles of clothing, gives you a glimpse of Sitka life during the Russian-America period.

To the west lies Sitka's best-recognized landmark, **St Michael's Cathedral** (summer Mon–Fri 9am–4pm; tel: 907-747 8120; donation requested). The original cathedral on the site, which was Alaska's oldest church from the Russian era, was destroyed by fire in 1966. Fortunately, nearly all the icons were preserved, and the present church was built to replace it, strictly following the original design.

The **Russian Block House** is a replica of one of the three original structures that once separated the Russian and Tlingit segments of town following the Natives' return to Sitka around 1824. Close by is the **Alaska Native Brotherhood Hall** (235 Katlian Street), and the **Sheet'ka Kwaan Naa Kahidi Tribal Community House** (456 Katlian Street; tel: 888-270 8687; charge for tours and dance performances; www.sitkatours. com), which host colorful Native dance performances and have a gift shop featuring Native artwork.

Castle Hill, on the National List of Historic Places, is just south, across Lincoln Street. In addition to being the site of the 1867 Russian/US transfer ceremony, it is the former location of Baranof's Castle, built in 1837 and destroyed by fire in 1898.

Out of Town

The **Fortress of the Bear** (May–Sep daily 9am–5pm; tel: 907-747 3550; charge; www.fortressofthebear.org), a rescue center for orphaned bears, 5 miles (8km) from the city center, provides the possibility to observe them in their natural habitat from a large viewing platform.

To take in the sights outside Sitka, consider a wildlife cruise to see humpback whales, sea otters, sea lions, and eagles. Birders would enjoy a trip to **St Lazaria Island** ⑮, part of the **Alaska Maritime National Wildlife Refuge** (www.fws.gov/refuge/alaska_maritime), at the mouth of Sitka Sound, which is home to thousands of seabirds, including comical tufted puffins. Additional exploration options include diving, flightseeing, and kayaking in Sitka's spectacular surroundings.

The bright lights of Sitka

Ship in the Tracy Arm fjord, near Juneau

NORTHERN PANHANDLE

The northern portion of Alaska's Inside Passage, which is considerably more rugged than the southern half, is studded with glaciers and icefields, crowned by the wonders of Glacier Bay National Park. The area also features some of Alaska's best whale-watching, especially in Icy Strait.

JUNEAU

The central area of Alaska's small state capital, **Juneau** ⑯, crowds up against steep mountain slopes in a compact network of narrow streets and alleys leading to museums, galleries, and bars.

Now home to 34,000 residents, it's a far cry from the rough camp where gold was discovered by Joe Juneau and Richard Harris in 1880. In 1959, when Alaska became the 49th state of the US, government had already taken over the economic niche once held by mining, and since then, it has grown from a waterfront community around the former mining sites into a growing city spreading for miles to the north and south. Not only is it the only US capital not accessible by road (which, incidentally, has led to calls for moving the capital to Anchorage), but it's also the only one to border a foreign country.

Downtown and Dock Area

For cruise ship passengers, **Marine Park Ⓐ**, overlooking the dock and wharf area, serves as a lively and welcoming introduction to Juneau. This is where half the city eats lunch on sunny days, and street vendors serve up snacks ranging from fried halibut and hot dogs to tacos and spring rolls. The **Travel Juneau Visitor Information Center Ⓑ** (daily May–Sep 8am–5pm; tel: 888-581-2201; www.traveljuneau.com), opposite the cruise-ship terminal, offers city maps and information on tours.

The **State Library, Archives, and Museum (SLAM) Ⓒ** (daily 8.30am–5.30pm; tel: 907-465 2901; charge; http://museums.alaska.gov) greets visitors with a towering spruce tree and a large floor map of Alaska. To the left of the lobby, you will find Inuit culture is represented by small, intricate ivory carvings and a huge 40ft (12m) *umiak*, or skin boat, of the type that were used for whale- and walrus-hunting along the ice floes of the Arctic Ocean. Southeast Alaska's Native

Patsy Ann

A statue of a bull terrier, *Patsy Ann* (who lived from 1929–42), sits on the wharf in Juneau to greet disembarking cruise ship passengers. In 1934 she was dubbed 'Official Greeter of Juneau, Alaska' by Mayor Isadore Goldstein in recognition of her uncanny ability (especially as she was stone deaf) to anticipate the arrival of every ship.

heritage is reflected in a community house re-creation, complete with totemic carvings, and interior Alaska's Athabascan culture is represented with a birch bark canoe, weapons, and bead-decorated moose-hide garments. The museum also displays gold rush memorabilia, Russian-era Orthodox Christian exhibits, including precious coins, priests' raiments, and the first US flag to be flown over Alaska, on October 18, 1867.

Along South Franklin Street, you'll find art galleries and shops selling Alaskan ivory, jade, totemic wood carvings, and leatherwork, as well as Juneau's best known bar, the fun but slightly cheesy **Red Dog Saloon D** (www.reddogsaloon.com). Further up the street, the tiny **St Nicholas Russian Orthodox Church E** (Mon–Thu 8.30am–4.30pm, Fri–Sun noon–4.30pm; donation requested; http://stnicholasjuneau.org), constructed in 1894 at the request of Tlingit chief Ishkhanalykh, provides a picturesque, onion-domed, and octagon-shaped glimpse into Russian colonial influence on the Native Tlingit people.

Alaska's **State Capitol Building F** (Mon–Fri 8.30am–5pm Sat–Sun 9am–4pm; tours every half hour in summer), on Fourth Avenue, built in the 1930s, is more practical office building than the typically stately domed capitol buildings in other states. In true Alaskan fashion, a 2004 design competition for a new, more impressive capitol building yielded lots of unworkable designs, including the winning egg-shaped fantasy, and the project was summarily abandoned.

The **Juneau-Douglas City Museum G** (Mon–Fri 9am–6pm, Sat–Sun 10am–4.30pm; tel: 907-586-3572; free; www.juneau.org/library/museum/index.php) focuses on the city's fishing and gold-mining history, and provides a free map of Juneau's nationally registered historic buildings and totem poles.

Few visitors will want to miss the steep ride in the gondola up the **Mount Roberts Tramway H** (tel: 907-461 8726; http://

mountrobertstramway.com), that climbs nearly 2,000ft (610m) in six minutes. At the top, you're rewarded with spectacular views, a visitors' center, a couple of gift shops, scores of hiking trails, a theater, and a restaurant overlooking the entire city. It begins from South Franklin Street, near the dockside.

North of Town and Mendenhall Valley

The well-known **Mendenhall Glacier** ⑰ is best viewed from the US Forest Service information center (tel: 907-586 8800; www.fs.usda.gov/tongass/), in the Mendenhall Valley 13 miles (21km) north of town. The face of the glacier is about a mile (1.6km) from the visitor center, which overlooks frigid Mendenhall Lake and its load of calved icebergs. The ice you see here has flowed down from the Juneau Icefield, a 1,500 sq mile (3,885 sq km) expanse of ice and snow that extends past the Canadian border.

The popular **Alaskan Brewing Company** (brewery Mon–Fri 8am–5pm, giftshop and tasting room Mon–Sat 11am–6pm; tel: 907-780 5866; www.alaskanbeer.com) conducts brewery tours and complimentary tastings of its award-winning brews, including seasonal brews and limited edition beers. A photo ID is required.

Quirky and fun, the **Glacier Gardens Rainforest**

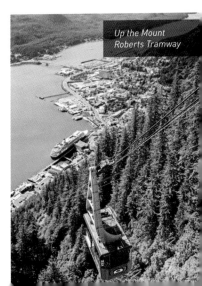

Up the Mount Roberts Tramway

Adventure (daily 9am–6pm; tel: 907-790 3377; charge; www.glaciergardens.com) takes visitors on a tour up the slopes by open shuttle vehicle through rainforested botanical gardens to an eagle's nest and a panoramic viewpoint overlooking Taku Inlet and Gastineau Channel. Visitors especially love the unique and whimsical 'flower towers', upended tree stumps turned into flower planters.

Juneau Icefield

Helicopter adventures to the vast **Juneau Icefield** ⓲ are weather-dependent, but if you're fortunate enough to have clear weather, don't miss it. All flights include impressive aerial views of the Taku Glacier and a landing on the expansive ice. Some also feature a dogsled trip from the Norris Glacier ice camp, where participants learn to mush a team of Iditarod sled dogs. Alternatively, try glacier hiking; operators supply a guide and equipment – boots, crampons, ice axes, and so forth – for a two-hour trek and even a little ice climbing.

Ice climber in the Juneau Icefield

Taku Inlet and Glacier

A popular shore excursion is the Allen Marine Tours (tel: 907-789 0081; www.allenmarinetours.com) trip to dramatic **Taku Glacier** ⓳, east of Juneau.

This advancing river of ice currently measures 37 miles (59km) long and 5 miles (8km) wide and threatens to dam the adjacent Taku River and form a lake. The trip begins by high-speed water-jet-powered catamaran to a World War II-era ship anchored in the impressive Taku Inlet fjord. Because the glacier face sits behind a shallow, shifting sandbar, the trip from this point to the ice is done by hovercraft, an amphibious vehicle which floats on a cushion of air over the water, ice, sand, and vegetation.

Icefields and Glaciers

Icefields are formed when snow builds up between mountain slopes and compresses beneath the increasing weight into an expanse of ice. When the edges of the icefield reach a critical weight, ice begins to flow downhill in river-like formations known as glaciers, which in turn grind and gouge out steep-sided valleys and, in some cases, spill into the sea and create fjords.

GLACIER BAY NATIONAL PARK

Encompassing 3.3 million acres (1.3 million hectares) at the northern end of the Alaska Panhandle, **Glacier Bay National Park and Preserve 20** (tel: 907-697 2627, www.nps.gov/glba) offers visitors unparalleled views of tidewater glaciers and the chance to explore the rich ecosystems that surround them. The focus of this wild national park is on the sea and the glacier views from it, so it makes sense that most visitors to Glacier Bay arrive on cruise ships, but there is no docking within the park. Often, National Park rangers will ride along on board to provide interpretative lectures on the park's wildlife, vegetation, ecosystems, and other natural features and surroundings.

Cruise ship passengers admiring Glacier Bay National Park

With a variety of environments, the park provides a rich overview of Alaskan wildlife, from humpback whales and Arctic peregrine falcons to common harbor seals, sea otters, black and brown bears, mountain goats, marmots, and bald eagles. In addition, 16 massive tidewater glaciers – including the frequently-viewed Margerie, Grand Pacific, Johns Hopkins and Muir Glaciers – flow down from the 15,300ft (4663m) **St Elias and Fairweather Ranges** to plunge into the icy fjords to form jagged icebergs that front the ice-scoured rock walls, saltwater beaches, and protected coves. **Bartlett Cove**, the park's main development, occupies an area dominated by coastal western hemlock and Sitka spruce, with bald eagles often observed soaring overhead.

Over time, the glaciers that created Glacier Bay have retreated and advanced due to climatic fluctuations. Early explorers Captains Cook, La Pérouse, and Vancouver observed the glacier face at the mouth of the bay in 1778, 1786, and 1794, respectively, but when naturalist John Muir visited in 1879, the ice had retreated 32 miles (51km) to a point near what is now the mouth of **Muir Inlet**. Ninety years later, the Muir Glacier had receded another 24 miles (39km) and today, the bay is more than 65 miles (105km) long. This glacial retreat has created a scientific testing laboratory for studying the arrival and colonization of new species in areas formerly covered by glacial ice.

As one of the world's largest marine sanctuaries, Glacier Bay has seen controversy regarding the number of cruise ships in the summer months. While some environmentalists want to ban large ships altogether, claiming that they damage the ecosystem, others argue that the cruise ships allow the largest possible numbers of people to enjoy the park with very little direct impact on the environment. Currently, access permits are limited to 153 ship visits from June to August and 92 in May and September combined. Currently, Princess, Holland America, Norwegian, Carnival and Crystal, plus several small companies, are permitted to enter the park.

ICY STRAIT POINT (HOONAH)

In search of a new cruising port in Southeast Alaska, operators discovered the long-ignored Native fishing port of **Hoonah** and the cannery at **Icy Strait Point** ㉑ near the mouth of Port Frederick on Chichagof Island. Not only is it a short cruise west of Juneau, it's also not far from the entrance to world-renowned Glacier Bay. To the site's existing attractions – wilderness, Native culture, Russian heritage, and ample wildlife viewing opportunities – it was decided to add a touch of adrenalin adventure in the form of what was – at its time of construction – the world's longest zipline. At present, the 5,330ft (1,625m)-long

The unmistakable Hammer Museum in Haines

Icy Strait Point ZipRider (summer daily 8am–5pm; tel: 907-789 8600; www. ziprider.com) is the world's sixth longest, but that in no way diminishes its incredible setting or the thrill of descending the 1,300ft (400m) at 60mph (100kph) from the summit of Hoonah Mountain to near sea level.

The zipline is open to anyone weighing between 90 and 275lbs (41 and 125kg). Along the 45-minute route up the mountain, drivers provide running commentary about Hoonah and its Tlingit heritage, but at 1300ft, you're fastened into a harness which allows your hands to be free for filming during the experience. And while you're zipping down at full speed, don't stress: a safe, brake-activated landing awaits at the bottom terminal.

Visitors who aren't up for the zipline can choose from whale-watching tours, wildlife tours, kayaking, ATV expeditions, fishing trips, a Tlingit Cultural tour, and a relaxing tour of the village on foot or by bus.

HAINES

With the exception of a handful of Holland America, Seabourn, and Princess ships, and some small lines, most cruise lines choose to dock at Skagway instead of **Haines** ㉒ (but it's possible to visit Haines on a shore excursion *from* Skagway). That means those who do land here will have fewer shore amenities, but will also find opportunities for a more personal welcome to a city whose setting may be America's most spectacular. Backed up by glaciated sawtooth peaks, Haines' claims to fame are its small-town ambience and its attraction for migrating bald eagles. Eagles are visible for most of the summer, but in mid-November – outside of cruising season – hundreds of them congregate to fish along the Chilkat River in the **Alaska Chilkat Bald Eagle Preserve** ㉓ north of the town.

Downtown and Dock Area

Several worthwhile sites lie within an easy walk of the docks. **Fort William H. Seward**, the first US government military post in Alaska, was built in 1904. In rather stark contrast to Haines' rustic frontier motif, this collection of stately, white clapboard structures surrounds the open space that served as the central parade grounds. The fort was decommissioned in 1947, and today, the atmospheric historical buildings serve as private homes, accommodations establishments, art galleries, and restaurants. There's also a Tlingit clan house and a collection of totem poles in the former Parade Ground.

The quirky and worthwhile **Hammer Museum** (Mon–Fri 10am–5pm, Sat 10am–2pm; tel: 907-766 2374; charge; www.hammermuseum.org) exhibits over 2,000 historic (and new) hammers used throughout the world for a dizzying array of purposes. As oddball as it sounds, this unique collection is certain to impress!

The **Sheldon Museum and Cultural Center** (Mon–Fri 10am–5pm, Sat–Sun 1–4pm; tel: 907-766 2366; charge; www.sheldonmuseum.org) showcases Haines' pioneer history exhibits as well as those of early Native Tlingit culture.

The **American Bald Eagle Foundation** (Mon–Sat 9am–5pm; tel: 907-766 3094; charge; www.baldeagles.org) museum features unique natural history dioramas, along with live bald eagle displays. Outside are nine enclosures housing a variety of raptors. The center is a non-profit educational foundation dedicated to the protection and preservation of bald eagle habitats, with daily live bird presentations in the summer.

Out of Town

At the village of Klukwan, 22 miles up the Chilkat River from Haines, you can experience the traditions, dance, and culture of the Chilkat Tlingit people at the **Jilkaat Kwaan Heritage Center** ㉔ (Mon–Fri 10am–4pm, Sat 1–4pm; tel: 907-767 5485; charge; www.jilkaatkwaanheritagecenter.org).

Several local companies offer shore excursions, which include **jet-boating** the Chilkat River with Chilkat River

Skagway's architecture recalls the Gold Rush era

Adventures (www.jetboatalaska.com) and **rafting** with Eagle Preserve Floats (www.raftalaska.com) or the Haines Rafting Company (www.hainesrafting.com). Other options will take you fishing and wildlife-viewing at Chilkoot Lake, deep sea fishing for salmon and halibut, or cycling, hiking, golfing, and photographing in Haines' scenic hinterlands.

SKAGWAY

There's no other Alaskan town quite like **Skagway** ㉕, which combines history, rusticity, and natural beauty at the northern end of the Inside Passage. Offering a range of exciting shore excursions, Skagway may seem to be a purpose-built cruise port, but in fact, it's one of Alaska's most interesting historical towns. It was from here in 1897–98 that the Gold Rush prospectors assembled their grubstakes in preparation for the long, arduous trek over the Chilkoot Trail to Bennett Lake and the Yukon River, which would carry them to the Klondike goldfields. Today, many of the historic buildings still stand, and the 1,000 or so residents cater to crowds of tourists, largely made up of cruise passengers. It's safe to say that it will be a highlight of any Alaska cruise.

Downtown and Dock Area

Skagway's center of activity starts at the docks and continues up along Broadway Street, where more than 60 gold rush-era buildings still stand. Many of these now house restaurants, saloons, hotels, art galleries, ice-cream parlors, and other businesses, some staffed by people in gold rush period dress.

The **Klondike Gold Rush National Historic Park Visitor Center** (daily May–Sep 8.30am–5.30pm; tel: 907-983 2921; www.nps.gov/klgo) contains a small museum with informative talks, a Gold Rush film, and free walking tours of the district. The Klondike National

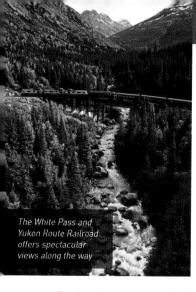

The White Pass and Yukon Route Railroad offers spectacular views along the way

Historic Park itself takes in the Skagway historic district, the ghost town of Dyea, the Chilkoot Trail, and also the Pioneer Square unit in Seattle, WA (see page 30).

Nearby, on the corner of Third Avenue and Broadway Street, the **Mascot Saloon** (daily May–Sep 8.30am–5.30pm; free), built in 1898, has some well-displayed exhibits which conjure up the rough, tough atmosphere of the saloon's heyday.

The **Arctic Brotherhood Hall** (www.arcticbrotherhood.com), covered with thousands of pieces of driftwood, is now the home of Skagway's **Convention and Visitors Bureau** (Mon–Fri 8am–5pm; tel: 907-983 2854; www.skagway.com).

At the corner of Fourth and Broadway is the restored **Pantheon Saloon**, which houses the **Junior Ranger Activity Center** (May–Sep Mon–Fri 10am–noon, 1–3pm) with hands-on gold-rush themed activities for children.

East along Fifth Avenue is **Moore Homestead Cabin** (May–Sep 10am–4.30pm), built by the city's founder and his son in 1887 and transferred to this spot when stampeders trampled over their land. Next door is the **Frye-Bruhn Warehouse**, part of an Alaska-wide meat-packing empire which used refrigeration system to preserve meat for prospectors and commercial clients. It's the only non-restored Gold Rush-era building in Skagway.

On the corner of Broadway Street and Sixth at **Eagle's Hall,** the **'Skagway in the Days of '98' show** (www.thedaysof98show. com) re-creates the Soapy Smith story nightly with an hour of live ragtime music and simulated gambling.

At the end of Seventh Avenue, in the century-old **City Hall**, is the **Skagway Museum and Archives** (Mon–Fri 9am–5pm, Sat 10am–5pm, Sun 10am–4pm; tel: 907-983 3420), with an array of historic artifacts, including a display of historic railcars.

White Pass and Yukon Route Railroad

Construction on the **White Pass and Yukon Route Railroad** ㉖ (tel: 907-983 2217; www.wpyr.com) began in the middle of Broadway Street on May 28, 1898, and by 1900, the 100-mile (160km) narrow-gauge line to Whitehorse, Yukon Territory, was completed. By providing an easy route to the gold fields, it turned the former city of Dyea, just over the hill from Skagway, into a ghost town. Today, the railroad conducts scenic excursions for sightseers and hikers, with spectacular mountain and canyon views along the entire route. Recommended trips run to 2,890ft (880m) White Pass Summit, or to Fraser in British Columbia, Canada (passport required), along the route to the Klondike gold fields.

Soapy Smith

Jefferson Randolph 'Soapy' Smith, Skagway's famous outlaw, won the allegiance not only of prostitutes and gamblers, but also of bankers, editors, and church builders. When one of his gang robbed a miner, Soapy refused to return the gold and he died while trying to break up the lynch mob. To book a tour of **Jeff Smith's Parlor Museum**, visit www.recreation.gov.

Out of Town

A worthwhile and adventurous tour, the **Grizzly Falls Zipline** (www.skagwayshoretours.com), begins 11 miles (18km) from Skagway, in the historic ghost town of **Old Dyea** , at the foot of the Chilkoot Trail, of which little remains but an old false front and some dock pilings. The route then makes a thrilling forest and waterfall circuit beginning with a Unimog slog up a muddy trail followed by 11 forest ziplines and four swinging suspension bridges.

Another highly acclaimed shore excursion, the **Glacier Point Wilderness Safari** (www.skagwayshoretours.com), heads into the wilderness through soaring glaciated peaks, temperate rainforests, and North America's deepest fjord – Lynn Canal – to Davidson Glacier, which calves into a deep blue lake. Throughout this combination high-speed boat ride, drive, a short hike, and a picnic on the beach, guides provide natural history commentary.

HUBBARD GLACIER (YAKUTAT)

Unless the weather is being uncooperative, most cross-Gulf cruises call in at the face of **Hubbard Glacier**, near the village of Yakutat. The glacier face measure six miles (10km) wide and 400ft (122m) high, but its length is more impressive. When a block of ice calves off the glacier

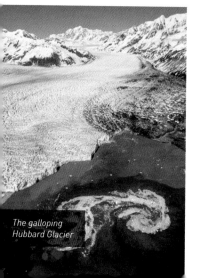

The galloping Hubbard Glacier

face, the snow that was compressed to create it has traveled 76 miles (122km) over the past centuries, beginning from 11,100 feet (3,400m) on the flanks of Mt Walsh, which rises above the Kluane Icefield in the Canadian Yukon.

Hubbard is North America's longest tidewater glacier (meaning it flows into the ocean), but unlike most tidewater glaciers, it is advancing. In the past 30 years, it has experienced two major surges large enough to choke off the entrance to Russell Fjord, turning this saltwater arm into a lake threatening to flood the village of Yakutat.

Cruise ships can often approach to within half a mile (800m) of the towering glacier face. The deep blue observed in the ice on a sunny day is created by light diffusion through crystals within the ice. On the ice floes formed by calving chunks, you'll often see basking seals, who take shelter there from hunting orcas.

> ### The Three Waves
>
> When watching a glacier calve, shipboard passengers are treated to a series of three waves. First, the sight of a huge chunk, falling silently – and seemingly in slow motion – from the wall, carried by light waves. Second, the cracking thunder of the event, carried on slower sound waves. Finally, the rocking of the ship created by the displacement of ice falling into water, which is carried on the even slower water waves.

SOUTH CENTRAL ALASKA

ANCHORAGE (GATEWAY TO SEWARD AND WHITTIER)

Alaska's 'big city', **Anchorage** ㉗, is the starting or ending point for all one-way Gulf of Alaska cruises. While the cruises arrive or depart from Seward, 120 miles (193km) away, or Whittier, 55 miles (88km) away, the international airport is in Anchorage, and you'll probably want to work it – as well as Whittier or Seward – into you pre- or post-cruise plans.

Although Alaska's largest city has been half-jokingly described as a 'beer can in the woods', this city of over 300,000, with all its attendant urban quirks, does present lots of worthwhile sites and an undeniably stunning setting between the Chugach Mountains and the cold waters of Cook Inlet.

Downtown Area

Those staying in Downtown Anchorage can easily explore this compact area on foot. A good starting point to pick up maps, brochures and other information is the **Log Cabin Visitor Information Center** Ⓐ (Jun–Aug daily 8am–7pm, late May and early Sep daily 8am–6pm; tel: 907-276 4118), in a 1954 log cabin on the corner of Fourth Avenue and F Street. Outside, note the 5,145lb (2,333kg) block of solid jade, the state's official gemstone. Information specific to national parks, national forests and other protected areas is best found at the **Alaska Public Lands Information Center** Ⓑ (summer daily 9am–5pm; tel: 907-644 3661; www.alaskacenters.gov), diagonally across the street.

At the **Old City Hall** Ⓒ, a classic 1930s construction next door to the log cabin, the lobby holds a display of photographs and other exhibits that trace the city's history. Along much of Fourth Avenue are lots of crowded souvenir shops offering T-shirts, Alaska knick-knacks, and Native art, including carved walrus ivory, soapstone, and baskets; be sure to ensure authenticity before purchase; genuine Native art will bear a silver hand logo. At Sixth Avenue and H Street,

The Anchorage skyline

the **Oomingmak Musk Ox Producers' Co-op** ⓓ (tel: 907-272 9225; www.qiviut.com) you can buy – or just admire – distinctive garments of musk ox wool, called qiviut, which are made in Inuit villages.

The glass and steel **Anchorage Museum** ⓔ (summer daily 9am–6pm; tel: 907-929 9200; charge; www.anchoragemuseum.org). Among the museum's permanent collections are the Alaska Gallery, with historical exhibits, and a fine selection of Native art and works by travelers, explorers and early residents, displayed in sky-lit galleries. The museum also houses the **Imaginarium Discovery Center** ⓕ (summer daily 9am–6pm; charge), a children's science center with a wealth of exhibits and hands-on exploration and learning about marine life, wetlands, and the solar system. Also part of the museum are the Smithsonian Arctic Studies Center, a planetarium, and a well-appointed café.

A few blocks west along Fifth Avenue, at M Street, is the historic **Oscar Anderson House Museum** (summer tours Tue–Sun noon–4pm; tel: 907-929 9870; www.aahp-online.net/oscar-anderson-house-museum.html), set in the attractive little Elderberry Park. Listed on the National Register of Historic Places, this is Anchorage's first wood-frame house, built by Swedish immigrant Anderson in 1915.

The **Saturday Market** (May–Sep Sat 10am–6pm, Sun 10am–5pm), occupies the parking lot on West Third Street between C and E streets. Accompanied by live music, hundreds of vendors hawk fresh Alaska produce, Native crafts, and a variety of takeaway food.

Around Town

East of the downtown area on the Muldoon Rd North exit from the Glenn Highway, the very worthwhile **Alaska Native Heritage Center** (summer daily 9am–5pm; tel: 907-330 8000; charge; www.alaskanative.net) showcases Alaska's Native cultures. Along the outdoor circuit, each Native group has its own section where you can learn about traditional customs and see master Native artists at work. Inside the center, Native artists and performers create and sell their works and stage theatrical and dance productions.

Near Tudor Road at the edge of the Far North Bicentennial Park, the **Alaska Botanical Garden** (4601 Campbell Airstrip Road; summer daily sunrise–sunset; tel: 907-770 3692; www.alaskabg.org) fills 110-acres (44.5-hectares) with over 1,000 species of native plants carefully tended and arranged into themed gardens.

Anchorage is great for urban hiking and cycling, with over 120 miles (190km) of paved paths. The best known route is the 11-mile (18km) **Tony Knowles Coastal Trail** (www.

anchoragecoastaltrail.com), which starts near Elderberry Park on Second Avenue and parallels the Cook Inlet shoreline to end at Kincaid Park. On the trail, cyclists share the pavement with hikers, joggers, rollerbladers, stroller-pushing parents, and the occasional moose. Along the way, it passes through **Earthquake Park** where, during the 1964 earthquake, 130 acres (52 hectares) of land slumped into the inlet and 75 homes were destroyed. By car, it's accessed along Northern Lights Boulevard.

Near the international airport is at **Lake Hood Air Harbor**, the world's busiest floatplane base and home of the very worthwhile **Alaska Aviation Heritage Museum** (mid-May–mid-Sep daily 9am–5pm; tel: 907-248 5325; charge; www.alaskaairmuseum.org), with hangars full of historic planes and displays on Alaska's unique and exciting aviation history. On clear summer days, there may be up to 600 take-offs and landings from Lake Hood and nearby Lake Spenard. To experience a taste of the Alaskan 'bush' (any place not accessible by road or sea), try a flight-seeing trip, which may include fishing, glacier-landing, and bear-viewing, or even a few nights at a well-appointed wilderness lodge. Hotels and cruise operators can help

Floatplane on Lake Hood

A large bull moose in Chugach State Park

organize excursions, and most remote lodges have websites with all pertinent details.

Chugach State Park

Immediately east of town is 495,000-acre (200,500-hectare) **Chugach State Park** ❷❽ (http://dnr.alaska.gov/parks/units/chugach). Its headquarters in the **Potter Section House State Historic Site** (Mon–Fri 10am–noon and 1–4.30pm; tel: 907-345 5014) also includes a small railroad museum and an old rotary snowplow. En route along the Seward Highway, it's worth walking the boardwalks of the **Anchorage Coastal Wildlife Refuge**, better known as Potter Marsh, which is home to an amazing variety of waterfowl.

The 3510ft (1,070m) **Flattop Mountain**, arguably the most climbed peak in Alaska, offers incredible views over Anchorage, the Alaska Range, Chugach Range, and the Cook Inlet. In summer, Flattop Mountain Shuttle provides transportation from downtown Anchorage to the Glen Alps Trailhead (charge for parking).

Another good place to begin a hike into Chugach State Park is the **Eagle River Nature Center** (summer Wed–Sun 10am–5pm; tel: 907-694 2108; charge for parking; www.ernc.org), 12 miles (19km) down Eagle River Road from the suburb of Eagle River. It's a highly worthwhile visit, with nature displays, salmon-viewing platforms, sheep-spotting scopes, great mountain views, excellent nature hikes, and the chance to see wildlife in its natural habitat.

Eklutna

About 20 miles (32km) out the Glenn Highway from Anchorage lies the tiny Native community of **Eklutna** ㉙, which was founded in 1650 as the first Dena'ina Athabascan settlement along Knik Arm. Anchorage's oldest building may well be the **St Nicholas Russian Orthodox Church**, which is part of **Eklutna Village Historical Park** (summer Mon–Sat 10am–5pm; services held Thu and Sat 5pm, Sun 9am; tel: 907-688 6026; www.eklutnahistoricalpark.org). It was constructed with hand-hewn logs, and the colorful spirit houses that surround it recall the Natives' historical interaction with Russian cultural influences. These small wooden structures, each with a three-bar Russian Orthodox cross, were placed over traditional graves and contained personal items thought to help the spirit in the afterlife.

⊙ MOOSE

If Alaska has a mascot, it's surely the ungainly, lumbering moose, and any sort of tourist paraphernalia you can name is available in moose motifs. Standing up to 10ft (3m) high and weighing as much as 1,600lbs (725kg), moose live anywhere in Alaska where there are trees to eat, including urban neighborhoods in Anchorage, Fairbanks, and other cities and towns. They're actually responsible for more human injuries than bears are, so if you see a moose – either in the woods or strolling down the sidewalk – be sure to give it a wide berth.

Catch of the day in Seward

WHITTIER

The port of **Whittier** ③⓪, with just over 200 people, is the start or end of cruises with the Princess and Crystal lines. In this odd little place with a spectacular waterfall-flanked setting on Prince William Sound, most residents occupy a single World War II-era high-rise, developed when the army used its ice-free harbor for a strategic fuel dump. When the town became an important military port, troops blasted tunnels through the Chugach Mountains to connect with the Alaska Railroad depot at Portage. Today, the tunnel is also used by the road connecting Whittier to the Seward Highway and Anchorage. Cruise lines run buses and rail cars between Whittier and Anchorage via Portage and Alyeska/Girdwood.

Along the way between Anchorage and Whittier, it's worth stopping in Portage at the **Alaska Wildlife Conservation Center** ③① (May–Aug daily 8.30am–7pm, Sep daily 9am–6pm; tel: 907-783 2025; www.alaskawildlife.org), a rehabilitation center where it's easy to pick up photos of moose, bears, and other wildlife. Another worthwhile spot in Portage is the **Begich-Boggs Visitors' Center** (late May–mid-Sep daily 9am–6pm; tel: 907-783 2326), with displays on the Chugach National Forest, a gift shop, and boat cruises across Portage Lake to the face of beautiful Portage Glacier.

From Whittier itself, **Prince William Sound Cruises and Tours** (tel: 907-777 2852; www.princewilliamsound.com) conducts the enormously popular **26 Glacier Cruise** into the surrounding fjords, named for major US colleges, where tidewater glaciers produce sudden, percussive, cracking sounds followed by thunderous roars as massive chunks of ice break loose and crash into the sea. For a meal in Whittier, don't miss what many Alaskans consider the world's best halibut and chips at the atmospheric **Varly's Swiftwater Seafood Café** (tel: 907-472 2550; www.swiftwaterseafoodcafe.com).

SEWARD

Passengers embarking on or disembarking from an Alaska cruise at **Seward** ㉜ (population 2,700) are typically shuttled by bus or train along spectacularly scenic routes to or from Anchorage with little or no time in this small, friendly, and attractive port community. That's a shame, because it enjoys

⊙ THE 1989 EXXON VALDEZ OIL SPILL

On March 24, 1989, the huge tanker *Exxon Valdez* hit a submerged rock reef in Valdez Arm of Prince William Sound on March 24 1989, releasing 11 million gallons (42 million liters) of crude oil into the water. The oil eventually spread along 1,100 miles (1,770km) of formerly pristine shoreline, causing an ecological disaster. At least 300,000 seabirds, 2,000 otters and countless other marine animals died as a result. Exxon spent US$2 billion cleaning up in the first year alone. The fishing industry has now largely recovered, and visitors to the Sound still see abundant wildlife, but there's evidence that some species, including orcas, have not yet recovered from the spill's toxic effects.

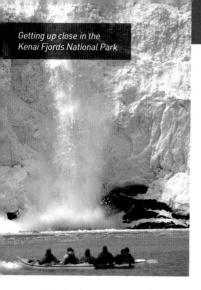

not only a spectacular setting at the head of Resu-
rrection Bay, but it's also
the jumping-off point for
visits to **Kenai Fjords
National Park** and a venue
for kayak rentals and sailing, whale watching and
fishing charters.

Downtown and Dock Area

Seward enjoys a compact,
rustic, and picturesque
downtown area, but there
are few must-see attrac-
tions apart from the
Alaska SeaLife Center (May–Aug Mon–Thu 9am–9pm, Fri–Sun
8am–9pm, Mar and Sep daily 10am–5pm; tel: 907-224-6300;
charge; www.alaskasealife.org). Overlooking Resurrection Bay,
it combines marine research and wildlife rescue with windows
onto the marine environment in the Gulf of Alaska. With a
series of aquariums, touch tanks, and other enclosed habitats,
visitors enjoy close-up views of Stellar sea lions, saltwater fish
species, shore birds, and life in tidal pools.

Kenai Fjords National Park

Seward is the gateway and headquarters for **Kenai Fjords
National Park** ㊳, designated in 1980. Above a series of rag-
ged coastal fjords rise rugged coastal ranges capped by glaciers and icefields. Most visitors see the park from the decks of
day cruises run by several Seward operators. These head out
Resurrection Bay from Seward's small boat harbor to Aialik

and Northwestern Fjords accompanied by porpoises, sea otters, sea lions, humpback whales, orcas, whales, puffins, bald eagles, and other wildlife.

A main destination, in the middle of Resurrection Bay, is Fox Island, which once served as a hermitage for iconic illustrator Rockwell Kent and is now used for well-attended salmon bakes on cruises with **Kenai Fjords Tours** (1304 Fourth Avenue; tel: 907-224 8068; www.kenaifjords.com) The longer half-day or full-day cruises typically include close-up views of calving glaciers.

The only vehicle access to the park is along Exit Glacier Road, immediately northwest of Seward, which leads to **Exit Glacier ㉞**. The glacier face lies less than a mile (1.6km) from the parking lot along a trail that can be hiked on your own or with a ranger guide. Energetic hikers can tackle the extremely steep 6-mile (10km) round trip hike up to the vast **Harding Icefield ㉟**, an Ice Age remnant that measures 50 miles

⊙ ALASKA'S MARINE MAMMALS

Every Alaska cruise passenger wants to see whales, and in Southeast Alaska and the Gulf of Alaska, the chances are good. Humpbacks, orcas (killer whales), minke whales, and porpoises are frequently observed in the Inside Passage, Icy Strait, Glacier Bay, and Kenai Fjords. Belugas, white whales that inhabit Cook Inlet, are often observed in Turnagain Arm, along the route between Anchorage and Whittier or Seward. Few cruise passengers will see walruses or bowhead whales, which are concentrated in western Alaska, but harbor seals, sea otters, and Stellar's sea lions are frequently sighted in the Inside Passage, Prince William Sound, and sheltered sites on the Gulf of Alaska.

(80km) long and 30 miles (48km) wide. Trips can be planned at the **Park Service Information Center** (tel: 907-422-0500 or 907-422-0535; www.nps.gov/kefj), on Fourth Avenue near the Seward Small Boat Harbor.

OTHER ALASKA PORTS OF CALL

Several cruise lines – for example, Ponant, Holland America, Seabourn, Crystal, and Silversea – currently operate a variety of non-Inside Passage cruises that include Alaska on their itineraries. Among these are the expedition-style cruises through the Northwest Passage from the west coast of North America to Greenland or the East Coast of the US and Canada. Others run trans-Pacific cruises to Japan and the Russian Far East, cruises around the Bering Sea, or to islands in the Russian Arctic, especially Wrangel Island. These cruises – in addition to the Alaska Marine Highway's Southwest Alaska system – use a growing number of non-traditional ports of call, such as several on the Kenai Peninsula, Kodiak Island, the Alaska Peninsula, the Aleutian Islands, the Bering Sea Islands, and the Seward Peninsula.

HOMER

Homer ㊱, a mid-sized town with an artistic flavor, sits on **Kachemak Bay** and serves as a highway-accessible Alaska Marine Highway port for trips to Kodiak and the Aleutian Islands. It's best-known for the 5-mile (8km) **Homer Spit**, which extends into the bay and is home to the town's boat harbor, campgrounds, hotels, restaurants, fishing charters, and the **Salty Dawg Saloon**, a popular watering hole housed in a historic lighthouse-shaped building.

The **Homer Visitor and Information Center** (Mon–Sat 9am–5pm; tel: 907-235 7740; www.homeralaska.org) has

Homer is a pleasant little
town with an artistic bent

information on attractions, including halibut charters and
water taxis around Kachemak Bay. Not to be missed is the
Alaska Islands and Ocean Visitor Center (Jun–Aug daily 9am–
6pm, Sep Tue–Sun 10am–5pm; tel: 907-235 6546; free; www.
islandsandocean.org). In addition to innovative displays, it features guided walks around the slough, tide pools, and marine
discovery lab. Also worthwhile is the natural history oriented
Pratt Museum (summer daily 10am–6pm; tel: 907-235 8635;
charge; www.prattmuseum.org), which focuses on Kachemak
Bay marine life and details on the Exxon Valdez oil spill.

SELDOVIA

Across Kachemak Bay from Homer, **Seldovia** ㉜ is the first stop on
the Alaska Marine Highway route from Homer to Kodiak and the
Aleutian Islands. Originally a coal-mining village in the late 18th
century, it's now involved mainly in the fishing industry. Much of

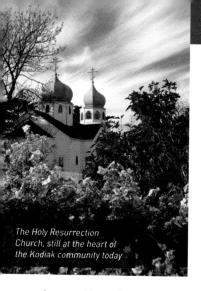

The Holy Resurrection Church, still at the heart of the Kodiak community today

the town's boardwalk area was destroyed in the 1964 earthquake, but it's still a pleasant and friendly little place to explore on foot while the ferry is docked.

KODIAK

With a name that immediately conjures up visions of its enormous, world-renowned brown bears, Kodiak island can be either a desolate, windswept, rain-pounded rock isolated from the rest of the world by fog or a shimmering emerald expanse of grassland and spruce, beneath snow-capped pinks glowing pink in the alpenglow. The city of **Kodiak** 🕸, with 6,130 people, many of whom are foreign workers in the canneries and fishing fleet, is a major Alaska Marine Highway port, as well as a port of call for cruise operators, including Holland America, Silversea, Seabourn (on its trans-Pacific route), and Crystal (on its Northwest Passage route).

Downtown and Dock Area

The best window on the island's Native Alutiiq culture is at the **Alutiiq Museum** (Tue–Fri 10am–4pm, Sat noon–4pm; tel: 907-486 7004; charge; www.alutiiqmuseum.org;). The **Baranov Museum** (summer Mon–Sat 10am–4pm; tel: 907-486 5920; charge; www.baranovmuseum.org), in Erskine House, North America's oldest Russian building, contains both Alutiiq and Russian artifacts and clothing, some from the Russian era.

There's also a 26ft (8m) Alutiiq *baidarka* (skin boat), covered in sea lion skins, dating from the late 1800s.

When the US bought Alaska from Imperial Russia, the Russian citizens eventually returned home, but the Russian Orthodox churches and its Alaska Native followers remained. The landmark blue onion domes of the **Holy Resurrection Church** are evidence that the Orthodoxy still plays a significant role in the Kodiak community, and is the predominant religion in the six villages around Kodiak Island. Inside the church, visitors can see many brilliantly colored icons, and are also welcome to attend services.

Around Kodiak Island

During World War II, Kodiak served as a major supply center for the Aleutian campaign, but all that remains of those war years are the moss-covered bunkers at **Fort Abercrombie State Historical Park** (tel: 907-486 6339; charge; dnr.alaska.gov/parks/units/kodiak), adjacent to beautifully spooky moss-covered spruce forests 4 miles (6.5km) from the city. On the adjacent headland is the **Kodiak Military History Museum**, full of military artifacts.

To get into the real wilderness – and to see the 12ft (3.5m) tall Kodiak brown bears – you'll need to visit the **Kodiak National Wildlife Refuge** (tel: 907-487 2600; http://kodiak.fws.gov), which can be reached only by air or sea.

Shore excursions are typically limited to deep-sea fishing, wildlife cruises to see whales, sea lions, otters and sea birds, and fishing industry tours that include the king crab fleet from *The Deadliest Catch* television program.

ALASKA PENINSULA

Alaska Peninsula ports, all within view of soaring volcanoes, are visited almost exclusively on the Alaska Marine Highway runs between Kodiak and Dutch Harbor.

Chignik ㊴. This tiny and beautifully situated Alaska Marine Highway port is surrounded by steep, rugged peaks, but offers little of interest except the views and the village itself.

Sand Point ㊵. This 19th-century Russian settlement is now inhabited mainly by Aleut and Scandinavian residents. Visitors on the short stop will have the opportunity to see bald eagles and perhaps even view the historic Russian Orthodox church.

King Cove ㊶. Known for its many bears and its picturesque Russian Orthodox church, this small, mainly Aleut village lives from hunting, fishing, and fish processing.

Cold Bay ㊷. Mainly an emergency landing field for trans-Pacific flights, Cold Bay is also home to the **Izembek National Wildlife Refuge** (tel: 907-532 2445; www.fws.gov/refuge/izembek), which serves as a crossroads for migrating waterfowl and shorebirds, including the entire world population of the black brant goose.

Dutch Harbor

THE ALEUTIAN ISLANDS

The lonely and wind-swept arc of volcanoes known as the **Aleutian Islands** extends south-west from the tip of the Alaska Peninsula in a 1,000-mile (1,600km) arc toward Asia. This home-land of the Aleut people is of particular interest for hikers, birdwatchers, and those interested in Aleutian cultural heritage and Alaska's most accessible World War II landmarks. Most islands lie within the **Alaska Maritime National Wildlife Refuge** (tel: 907-235 6546; www.fws.gov/refuge/alaska_maritime).

Several islands are ports of call for the Alaska Marine Highway, and are also visited by Silversea Expeditions. Celebrity, Crystal, and Holland America cruise ships also call in at Dutch Harbor/Unalaska on their trans-Pacific cruises.

False Pass . False Pass, on Unimak Island, anchors the channel between this easternmost of the Aleutian Islands and the Alaskan mainland. In the backdrop on this treeless emerald island tower the imposing Isanotski and Shishaldin volcanoes.

Akutan . Tiny Akutan village, on the island of the same name, is currently served only by the Alaska Marine Highway system. Huddled against steep mountains, it combines an Aleut population and an active fishing fleet. The main site of interest is the St Alexander Nevsky Russian Orthodox church.

Dutch Harbor/Unalaska . The 'capital' of the Aleutians, the port of Dutch Harbor, on Amaknak Island, and the adjacent village of Unalaska, on Unalaska Island, sit at the heart of the very treacherous Bering Sea king crab fishery, with rich Russian and Unangan (Aleut) roots. Despite the typically foul weather, its magical light, green treeless mountains, and misty volcanoes make this place a unique experience for visitors.

A worthwhile excursion climbs up **Mount Ballyhoo** in the **Aleutian World War II National Historical Park** (Wed–Sat 1–6pm; tel: 907-581 9944; www.nps.gov/aleu) to see the World War II bunkers used against the 1942 Japanese invasion of the island. The bunkers and the park visitors' center near the airport can be reached by taxi.

To learn about highlights of traditional Aleut culture, see the excellent **Museum of the Aleutians** (Tue–Sat noon–6pm;

tel: 907-581 5150; charge; www.aleutians.org) at Margaret Bay. In **Unalaska** (www.unalaska.info), across the whimsically-named Bridge to the Other Side from Dutch Harbor, the main attraction is the colorful Russian Orthodox **Church of the Holy Ascension** (tel: 907-981 3790 for an appointment to enter). It was originally constructed in 1827 but has gone through several renovations, most recently in 1990.

Attu Island ㊻. The westernmost island of the Aleutians, Attu was occupied by Japan during WWII and its Native Aleut population was subsequently evacuated. This end-of-the-world port lies 1,100 miles (1,800 km) from mainland Alaska, 208 miles (335km) from Russia's Commander Islands, and 4,800 miles (7,725km) from Washington DC. It serves as a port of call on Silversea Expeditions Russian Far East cruises.

BERING SEA ISLANDS

A popular US comedy program once lampooned former Alaska Governor and US Vice Presidential candidate Sarah Palin, claiming she'd said you could 'see Russia from her house'. In fact, Russia IS visible from Alaska (albeit not from Ms Palin's house), on both the Seward Peninsula and a handful of Bering Sea islands. Some of these are visited on Northwest Passage, Russian Far East, and Bering Sea Cruises, and other expedition-level cruises through the Bering Strait. The main players are Ponant and Silversea.

St Paul and the Pribilof Islands ㊼. Sometimes called the 'American Galápagos', the lonely and lovely Pribilof Islands are home to Arctic foxes, reindeer, fur seals, and 240 bird species, including two million nesting kittiwakes, fulmars, auklets, murres, cormorants, and other seabirds. It's also the only North American habitat for several Asian itinerant bird species, such as McKay's bunting. Ships call in at St Paul village,

which has a photogenic Russian Orthodox church. It's a port of call on Silversea Expeditions Bering Sea cruises.

St Matthew 48. Extremely remote and rarely visited, St Matthew is flanked by black gravel beaches and soaring 1000ft (330m) sea cliffs that attract nesting murres, kittiwakes, cormorants, and other sea birds.

St Lawrence 49. Two villages, Gambell and Savoonga, anchor the Siberian Yu'pik island of St Lawrence, which fiercely retains its Siberian cultural roots. Here, people still hunt bowhead whales, seals, and walrus, and engage in fishing, reindeer herding, and Native carving in walrus ivory and whalebone. The port is at Gambell, on the island's northwest cape, facing Russia's Chukchi Peninsula.

Little Diomede 50. The very last outpost of North America, Little Diomede village faces Russian Big Diomede, about two miles (3km) away, but unlike its Russian neighbor, it

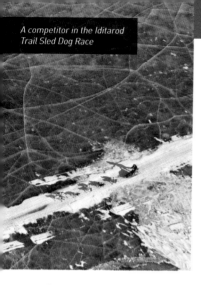

A competitor in the Iditarod Trail Sled Dog Race

does have a permanent Native population. Lying across the International Dateline, Big Diomede belongs not only to a different country, continent, and hemisphere, but also a different date.

NOME

Once a Wild West gold mining boomtown, **Nome** ❺❶ is now best known as the commercial hub of the vast Seward Peninsula and the finish line of the 1049-mile (1688-km) Iditarod Trail Sled Dog Race.

In 1898, the 'Three Lucky Swedes' found gold in Anvil Creek, and thousands of prospectors descended on this largest and rowdiest of Alaska gold rush towns. By 1900, Nome's population exceeded 20,000, including renowned frontier marshall and saloon-keeper Wyatt Earp. Many of the first arrivals, who came to pan and dredge the streams, camped on the town's black sand beaches, and before long, it was discovered that even the beach sand underfoot contained a richness of alluvial gold. Because no private claims could be made on the public beaches, it became a free-for-all, and the sands were turned over again and again to yield millions of dollars in gold. It was later discovered that even the ancient beaches beneath the sea were rich in gold deposits, and today, people still use floating dredges to dig, re-dig, and extract the latent wealth from the waters of Norton Sound.

Things to See and Do

Cruise ship passengers calling in at Nome will be greeted with several shore options. The Seward Peninsula offers all kinds of adventures – fishing, hiking, wildlife viewing, birding, and mountain biking, and soaking in hot springs – and roads connect Nome with other communities, including the remote Native village of **Teller** (population 237) and the ghost towns of **Council** and **Solomon**, where the most enigmatic attraction is **The Last Train to Nowhere**, the rusting hulk of a stranded gold-rush era train that's now frozen into the tundra muskeg.

In town, the small **Carrie McLain Museum** (May–Sep daily 10am–5pm; tel: 907-443 6630; charge) concentrates mostly on gold rush memorabilia, and visitors can learn how to operate a gold pan. Just outside the town languish several abandoned gold dredges, and several shops sell ivory carvings and other Native artwork.

Anyone with their own gold pan is welcome to pan the beach sands along the waterfront, but note that even during the heyday,

⊘ THE IDITAROD

Although the Iditarod – 'The Last Great Race' – is run in March, even summer visitors to Nome can appreciate the town's greatest modern claim to fame. This 1,049-mile (1,688km) dogsled race from Willow to Nome commemorates the life-saving diptheria serum run from Fairbanks in 1925, which due to bad weather had to be done by dogsled. After nine to 15 days on the trail, racing mushers and their teams are greeted in Nome with much fanfare as they pass beneath the 'burled arch' finish line along Front Street. In summer, the arch can be seen sitting in front of the Town Hall.

Alaska Marine Highway System ferry

the only folks making easy money were the gamblers, shysters, and ladies who relieved the miners of their hard-won fortunes.

THE ALASKA MARINE HIGHWAY

Sometimes called the 'poor man's cruise', the **Alaska Marine Highway System** ferries provide an adventurous alternative to the international cruise lines. The nine ferries of the system, operated by the State of Alaska, run year-round service between Bellingham, Washington (or Prince Rupert, British Columbia, Canada), and many of Alaska's coastal communities.

The beautiful trip between Bellingham and Alaska through British Columbia's Inside Passage follows roughly the same route as most cruises, but amenities are extremely basic and typically require booking at least six months in advance, especially for high-season cabins or vehicle space. Meals are available on the larger ferries and on longer runs, but the most basic and economical deck passage tickets involve using indoor reclining seats or camping out and picnicking in a heated deck-top solarium. It's also possible to put up a small free-standing tent on deck, but bring duct tape to secure it to the deck. Note that there's no access to vehicles when the ship is underway.

The entire run from Bellingham to Juneau takes three days, plus another two days to cross the Gulf of Alaska to Seward, with lots of opportunities for breaks in any of the towns and villages along the way. Unlike on a standard cruise, all the logistics must be worked out individually, and if you want to stop anywhere, you'll probably wind up traveling on multiple ships. Ferry timetables change from year to year and are available from the **Alaska Marine Highway System Reservations Office** (6858 Glacier Hwy, PO Box 112505, Juneau, AK 99811; tel: 800-642 0066 or 907-465 3941; email: dot.ask.amhs@alaska.gov; www.ferryalaska.com).

BELLINGHAM, WASHINGTON

The Bellingham Cruise Terminal, at the end of Chuckanut Dr (Fairhaven Parkway), is the 'Lower 48' departure point for the Alaska Marine Highway State Ferries. Be at the dock at least two hours prior to departure, especially if you're taking a vehicle. Last minute supplies are available in the Fairhaven Shopping Center near the ferry dock.

SOUTHEAST ALASKA ROUTES

Beginning in Bellingham, Washington, north of Seattle, the Alaska Marine Highway connects the 'Lower 48' with Southeast Alaska. The route north follows the Inside Passage along British Columbia's west coast, stopping en route at Prince Rupert, British Columbia, and entering Alaska at the 'First City', Ketchikan.

A bald eagle, national bird of the United States

Within Southeast Alaska, several ferries run between Ketchikan, Wrangell, Petersburg, Juneau, Haines, and Skagway. Others make a side trip west to Sitka, with possible stops in the small villages of Kake, Angoon, Tenakee Springs, Gustavus, Pelican, and Hoonah (Icy Strait Point). High-speed ferries run between Juneau, Haines, and Skagway, and small runs connect Ketchikan with Metlakatla. Of these, only Haines and Skagway have highway access.

Note that all passengers traveling between Bellingham and Alaska on this route must carry a passport that allows entry into Canada, even those not disembarking in Prince Rupert.

Another ferry company, **Inter-Island Ferries** (PO Box 470 Klawock, AK 99925; tel: 907-225 4848; email: reservations@inter islandferry.com; www.interislandferry.com), links Ketchikan with beautiful **Prince of Wales Island**, which is the largest island in the Alexander Archipelago and has the most extensive road system in all of Southeast Alaska. A vehicle is essential for visits to visit Prince of Wales Island.

PRINCE WILLIAM SOUND ROUTES

Sheltered Prince William Sound is a compact, glacier-studded expanse of water that provides lots of scope for adventure and sightseeing. In the summer, the main ports of **Whittier** (see page 84), **Valdez** 52 and **Cordova** 53, are accessed by ferry every day or two. These routes cut off a long drive to Valdez, and also provide the only vehicle access to Cordova. Along the way, you'll be treated to views of numerous glaciers and forested islands, with excellent chances of seeing whales, bald eagles, and other wildlife. From Cordova, there is road access to the world-class birdwatching at Alaganik Slough, 22 miles (35km) from town.

SOUTHWEST ALASKA ROUTES

The Southwest ferry routes connect Homer, Alaska, on the Kenai Peninsula, with this island city of Kodiak, plus the villages of Chignik, Sand Point, King Cove and Cold Bay on the Alaska Peninsula, and False Pass, Akutan, and Dutch Harbor/Unalaska, in the Aleutian Islands. Apart from Homer, none of these ports has highway access and the ferry provides both vehicle transport and a supply lifeline to these remote outposts.

For real adventure on the Alaska Marine Highway, nothing beats the run between Homer and Dutch Harbor/Unalaska in the Aleutian Islands. This week-long round trip follows a wilderness coast through some of the foulest weather and most unforgiving seas on earth, and it's not for the faint-hearted or easily seasick. But if you can imagine a volcanic peninsula and a chain of wild islands bathed in mist and suffused with an almost unearthly light, you're ready for this rewarding journey to what will seem like the ends of the earth.

PRE/POST-CRUISE EXCURSIONS

GIRDWOOD/ALYESKA

Technically a suburb in the Municipality of Anchorage, the small community of **Girdwood** 54 lies deep in the valley of

Glacier Creek, surrounded by an arc of glacier-crowned peaks and the waters of Turnagain Arm. Its main attraction, **Alyeska Resort** (tel: 907-751 2111; www.alyeskaresort.com), includes Alaska's best-known ski slopes, as well as a network of hiking and mountain biking trails, and a couple of dining options 2,200ft (670m) above the hotel at the top of a scenic gondola ride. The view from the top takes in myriad peaks, seven different glaciers, and glimmering Turnagain Arm below. In summer, the resort is known as a place to pamper yourself for a few days before or after a cruise.

The choice of tours includes whale-watching cruises from Seward; the **26 Glacier Cruise** (www.phillipscruises.com) on Prince William Sound; Alaska Railroad visits to Spencer Glacier for rafting or ice climbing; helicopter landings on a glacier; kayaking tours; guided hikes; wildlife-viewing at the **Alaska Wildlife Conservation Center** (see page 84) in Portage; and

⊘ THE ALASKA RAILROAD

The 470-mile (756km) Alaska Railroad, which connects Anchorage with Fairbanks to the north and Whittier and Seward to the south, offers excellent sightseeing opportunities, domed vista cars, and packaged excursions as possible cruise extensions. For information, contact the Alaska Railroad (tel: 907-265-2494/800-544-0552; www.alaskarailroad.com).

Princess and Holland America cruise passengers can avail themselves to those companies' luxurious and extremely popular domed cars that travel on the Alaska Railroad and connect the cruise ports of Seward and Whittier with tours to Anchorage, Denali National Park, Fairbanks, Talkeetna, and Prince William Sound.

a host of other options. After a day of exploring, you can enjoy Cajun cuisine at **The Double Musky** (www.doublemuskyinn. com), which is considered by many to be Alaska's finest dining.

TALKEETNA

Until recently, **Talkeetna** 🟤 served as a genuine small-town slice of Alaskana – it was in fact the inspiration for Cicely in the TV series *Northern Exposure* – but of

Picturesque Talkeetna

late, its charms have been 'discovered' by growing numbers of visitors, new residents, and developers. Nevertheless, Talkeetna remains quite rustic and picturesque, and it does have a front-row view of Denali, making it an ideal jumping-off point for climbers, flight-seers, and anyone seeking a relaxing getaway. Access for cruise extension passengers is either by tour bus or on the Alaska Railroad, which runs through the town.

In the 'downtown' area, renovated miners' cabins have been spruced up and converted into gift shops, lodgings, and restaurants, and the nearby **Talkeetna Alaskan Lodge** (tel: 800-808 8068; www.talkeetnalodge.com) offers clean, modern, and beautifully rustic post-and-beam style accommodations, complete with stunning Denali views. Princess Cruises also owns a lodge overlooking the Chulitna River about an hour north of Talkeetna, the **Mt McKinley Princess Wilderness Lodge** (tel: 907-733 2900; www.princesslodges.com/princess-alaska-lodges/

Spectacular Denali peak

mckinley-lodge), in **Denali State Park** (tel: 907-745 3975; www.
dnr.alaska.gov/parks/units/denali1.htm), which is used for staging cruise extension tours into Denali National Park.

Talkeetna also attracts visitors with fishing charters, river rafting adventures, several summer festivals, and flightseeing tours
over Denali. The Talkeetna Chamber (tel: 907-414 0376; www.
talkeetnachamber.org) happily provides tourist information.

DENALI NATIONAL PARK

At some 9,375 sq miles (24,500 sq km), **Denali National Park
and Preserve** ❺❻ (tel: 907-683 9532; www.nps.gov/dena) is
the third-largest national park in the United States, after
Wrangell-St. Elias and the Gates of the Arctic (both also in
Alaska). Presiding over it is North America's highest peak,
Denali ❺❼ (formerly Mount McKinley), part of the Alaska Range,
which divides the park into north and south portions.

The entire park is a wonderland of natural beauty, but visitors who hope to see Denali's undeniably spectacular peak will need a bit of luck. First, it's not visible from Denali Village, where most visitors stay, and secondly, it's normally obscured by cloud cover, but when it does appear, no one is disappointed. The best views from the south are from the town of Talkeetna and along the Parks Highway, and on the north side along Denali Park Road between the Eielson Visitors' Center and Wonder Lake.

The south side is popular with mountaineers and those on flightseeing tours, but most visitors go to the north side and travel along the **Denali Park Road**, which winds for 92 miles (148km) to Wonder Lake and the former village of Kantishna. Other notable sites in the park include the **Husky Homestead**, a training center for sled dogs, and the kid-friendly **Murie Science and Learning Center**, with hands-on exhibits and even a fossilized dinosaur footprint.

Most visitors on cruise extensions travel to Denali in one of the purpose-built domed rail cars along the Alaska Railroad and stay in one of the many hotels in **Denali Village** ⑱,

⊙ THE AURORA BOREALIS

Alaska is the best place in the US to view the aurora borealis, or northern lights, a solar-powered light show that occurs when charged particles from the sun collide with ions in the upper atmosphere. Unfortunately, summer visitors have almost no chance of seeing them, due to the perpetual daylight or 'midnight sun'. To see the aurora, cruise passengers will have the best chances traveling in late August or September and extending their trip to Denali National Park or Fairbanks (especially Chena Hot Springs).

The northern lights in Fairbanks

from where park visits are launched. Sightseeing along the park road is done on guided tours or on the green Visitor Transportation System shuttle buses, which stop whenever someone wishes to board or head off on a hike (except when wildlife is immediately visible). Along the park road are excellent chances for viewing wildlife, including moose, caribou, Dall sheep, grizzly bears, and a host of smaller animals. Note that private vehicles are prohibited except to access reserved campsites at Teklanika campground.

FAIRBANKS

Established in 1903 after a gold strike by prospector Felix Pedro, **Fairbanks** ⑨ – named for an Indiana senator who later became Vice President under Theodore Roosevelt – had its beginnings as a trading post, complete with a tent city, a few log houses, and wooden sidewalks over soggy muskeg. Beneath its workaday exterior, Fairbanks is now a lively city of friendly people who tend to appreciate more isolation than do their Anchorage counterparts. The city boasts the state's flagship university, the University of Alaska Fairbanks, and late in the summer season, it makes a good vantage point for viewing the aurora borealis.

Around Fairbanks

The **University of Alaska Fairbanks** (UAF), on a bluff overlooking the town, offers free guided walking tours (summer Mon–Fri 10am and 2pm; tel: 907-474 7021; www.uaf.edu/visituaf). On the campus, the **Museum of the North** (summer daily 9am–7pm; tel: 907-474 7505; charge; www.uaf.edu/museum) is one of Alaska's best, combining cultural artifacts, scientific equipment, and prehistoric objects extricated from the permafrost. There are also tours of the **Geophysical Institute** (tel: 907-474 7558; www.gi.alaska.edu), a world center for Arctic and aurora research, with a spectacular film on the aurora borealis.

Creamers Field (tel: 907-452 6152; donation requested; www.creamersfield.org) was originally Charles Creamers' dairy farm, started in 1920. The 250 acres (100 hectares) produced dairy products until it was purchased by the state in 1967 and set aside as a waterfowl refuge. It now boasts 2,000 acres (809 hectares) of wildlife habitat, and is known for the flocks of sandhill cranes who congregate here in the summer. Motoring enthusiasts will enjoy the nearby **Fountainhead Antique Auto Museum** (summer Sun–Thu 10am–8pm, Fri–Sat 11am–6pm; tel: 907-450 2100; charge; www.fountainheadmuseum.com), with more than 85 antique vehicles.

Riverboats have been used on the Chena and Tanana rivers since the Gold Rush, and continuing with that tradition, a prominent local family operates the 700-passenger sternwheeler *Discovery III* (tel: 907-479 6673; www.riverboatdiscovery.com)

The Denali Grand Slam

The aim of nearly all Denali visitors is to score a Denali Grand Slam, which means spotting at least one moose, caribou, Dall Sheep, and grizzly Bear AND the peak of Denali – all in one day.

Enjoying a dip in the Chena Hot Springs Resort

for excursions on the rivers, including a stop at a mock-up Athabascan village. Reservations are recommended.

Chena Hot Springs

East of Fairbanks, the Chena Hot Springs Road leads 56 miles (90km) through the beautiful Chena State Recreation Area to road's end at Chena Hot Springs. Along the way, several excellent hiking trails – Angel Rocks, Granite Tors, and Chena Dome - head into the hills, but most visitors aim for the well-appointed and eco-friendly **Chena Hot Springs Resort** ⑩ (tel: 907-451 8104; www.chenahotsprings. com). Fully developed for comfort, it's equipped for visits the year-round, and in late summer, it's one of the best venues for viewing the northern lights. Most alluring are the steaming hot-water pools of **Monument Creek Valley**, the indoor swimming pools, and the indoor and outdoor soaking facilities.

North Pole

The Fairbanks suburb of North Pole, 17 miles (27km) east of town, is best-known as the place where Christmas is celebrated year-round, with its holiday gift shop, **Santa Claus House** (summer daily 8am–8pm; tel: 907-488 2200; www. santaclaushouse.com), Santa's reindeer, and holiday-themed street names, like Snowman Lane and St Nicholas Drive. Every year they receive hundreds of thousands of letters addressed to Santa, 101 St Nicholas Drive, North Pole, AK 99705, and personal responses can be arranged by visitors to the site.

KATMAI NATIONAL PARK

Katmai National Park ❶ (tel: 907-246 3305; www.nps.gov/katm) lies 290 air miles (465km) from Anchorage, and most people access it on a day trip by floatplane from Anchorage, or commercial flight to King Salmon and then float plane or small boat to Brooks Camp, which is inside the park. The park is not accessible by road.

The main attraction is **Brooks Camp**, on **Naknek Lake**, where a large run of sockeye salmon each summer attracts dozens of brown bears to fish in the Brooks River, particularly at Brooks Falls. From the camp, several easy walks lead to safe raised viewing platforms where you can watch the bears fishing,

⊙ THE TRANS-ALASKA PIPELINE

Between the North Slope and Valdez, the Trans-Alaska Pipeline had to cross three mountain ranges, active fault lines, miles and miles of unstable muskeg (boggy ground comprised mostly of decaying vegetation) and the migration paths of wildlife, particularly caribou.

The pipeline was designed with all these factors in mind. To counteract the unstable ground and allow animal crossings, half the pipeline is elevated on supports, which hold the pipe – and the hot oil inside – high enough to keep it from melting the permafrost. To help the pipeline survive an earthquake, it was laid out in a zigzag pattern, so that it would roll with the earth instead of breaking up.

Brooks Camp bears in fishing action

catching, and devouring the salmon. In addition to the bears, moose, caribou, land otters, wolverines, martens, weasels, mink, lynx, foxes, wolves, muskrats, beavers, and hares all inhabit the park.

Visitors when the bears aren't around – or those on longer visits, will want to take a day tour from Brooks Camp to the **Valley of Ten Thousand Smokes**, which resulted from the eruption of Novarupta volcano in 1912. This massive geological event was heard over 750 miles (1,200km) away and caused massive earthquakes and landslips all over South Central Alaska. Once a desert of steaming fumaroles, the '10,000 Smokes' subsided decades ago, but volcanic ash, pumice, and heavier igneous rock produced over 40 sq miles (100 sq km) of otherworldly landscape, sculpted by wind and water. In 1916, the landscape's fiery desolation prompted researching botanist Robert Griggs to name one stream the **River Lethe**, in reference to the Greek mythological river that flowed into Hades.

LAKE CLARK NATIONAL PARK

One of Alaska's wildest national parks, little-visited **Lake Clark National Park ❷** makes an excellent and adventurous destination for one-day fly-in fishing, wildlife-viewing, and sightseeing trips by bush plane from Anchorage. The centerpiece is deep blue Lake Clark, 42 miles (68km) long, up to 860ft (262m) deep and covering 110 sq miles (285 sq km). The lake is surrounded by towering peaks, while over the ridges steam a couple of active volcanoes; Mt Redoubt erupted in a grand fashion as recently as 2009. Anglers come mainly for rainbow trout and salmon, but lake trout, pike, Dolly Varden, Arctic char, and Arctic grayling are also much sought species.

An oft-requested destination within the park is **Upper Twin Lake**, where in the 1960s homesteader Richard 'Dick' Proennicke hand-built a cabin and lived a reclusive lifestyle. His tale is told in the book *One Man's Wilderness: An Alaskan Odyssey*, by his friend Sam Keith, who based it on Proennicke's journals. The story was later made into an award-winning documentary film.

◎ GETTING THE PHOTO!

Those iconic photos you've seen of brown bears fishing for salmon in a waterfall were taken at Brooks Camp in Katmai National Park. The main salmon run – and therefore best viewing – is in late June and through much of July, but some bears are also around in late August and early September. Competition for access during the best viewing times can be fierce, so to score the classic photo will require a one-day fly-in tour from Anchorage, luck booking a room at Brooks Camp Lodge (tel: 800-544 0551; www.katmailand.com), or speed-dialing for a National Park cabin or campsite tel: 877-444 6777 or 518-885 3639; www.recreation.gov) when the permits are released in early January. For a list of permitted outfitters that access the park see www.nps.gov/akso/management/commercial_services_directory.cfm.

The main park office is in Anchorage (tel: 907-644 3626; www.nps.gov/lacl), with a field headquarters at **Port Alsworth** (tel: 907-781 2218) on Lake Clark's southeast shore. The only other public facilities are privately owned wilderness lodges catering mainly to hunters and anglers, including several at Port Alsworth, the entry point for many visitors.

OTHER DESTINATIONS

Cruise ship companies and other travel operators can organize excursions to just about any corner of Alaska that sparks your interest. The following worthwhile destinations provide opportunities to explore the lesser-known corners of the state without having to rough it.

Wrangell-St Elias National Park ⑬. The largest National Park in the US, this 13.2 million acre (5.3 million hectare) wilderness of mountains, glaciers, and wild rivers focuses on the copper rush ghost town of Kennecott and the tiny service center of McCarthy. At the turn of the 20th century, prospectors Jack Smith and Clarence Warner spotted a large green spot in the Wrangell Mountains which proved to be a fantastically rich copper deposit. The discovery sparked the construction of the 200-mile (320-km) Copper River & Northwestern Railroad, connecting the mining camp to the coastal town of Cordova.

When the mine closed in 1938 it had produced over 4.5 million tons of ore, worth US$200 million. At its peak, around 600 people lived at **Kennecott**, which included extensive milling operations as well as houses, offices and stores, a school, hospital, post office, dairy, and recreation hall. Just down the road, **McCarthy** sprang up around 1908 to provide Kennecott workers with saloons, pool halls, gambling rooms, and back-alley brothels.

Today, the park's greatest treasures lie in a wild and magnificent alpine world that includes four major mountain ranges – the St Elias, Chugach, Alaska, and Wrangell – and six of the continent's 10 highest peaks, including 18,008ft (5,490m) **Mount St Elias**, North America's fourth-highest mountain. A range of services are available in McCarthy and Kennecott, and hiking, flight-seeing tours and guided glacier walks provide relatively easy access to the surrounding wilderness.

View over to Mount Wrangell, Wrangell-St Elias National Park

Within the park, the hotel of choice is **Kennicott Glacier Lodge** (tel: 907-258 2350; www.kennicottllodge.com), which overlooks a vast glacier landscape in the historic Kennecott ghost town. Many visitors on cruise extensions stay a four-hour drive from Kennecott at the **Copper River Princess Lodge** (tel: 907-822 2000; www.princesslodges.com/princess-alaska-lodges/copper-river-lodge), which is near the very well-appointed park **Visitors' Center** (tel: 907-822 7250; www.nps.gov/wrst/index.htm) at Copper Center on the Richardson Highway.

The Dalton Highway and The North Slope. North America's ultimate road to adventure, the former Trans-Alaska Pipeline Haul Road, the supply route now known as the **Dalton Highway ⑥**, connects the tiny village of Livengood, north of Fairbanks, with the Prudhoe Bay oilfields. Following the Alaska

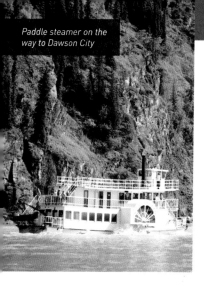

Pipeline through the boreal forests, it crosses the Arctic Circle and the Brooks Range, then slides between Gates of the Arctic National Park and the Arctic National Wildlife Refuge before descending across the vast tundra plains of the North Slope to end at Deadhorse, popularly known as **Prudhoe Bay**, on the icy Arctic Ocean coastline. In addition to the scenery, travelers along this route are likely to see a range of Arctic wildlife, from Arctic foxes and hares to moose, caribou, musk oxen and near the road's end, even polar bears.

From Fairbanks, the **Northern Alaska Tour Company** (tel: 800-474 1986; email: adventure@northernalaska.com; www.northernalaska.com) and other operators offer tours (or just transport) to the Prudhoe Bay oil fields, including a flight in one direction and an indescribably beautiful 500-mile (800km) mostly gravel road trip in the opposite direction. The price provides a night in the village of **Coldfoot** and another in Prudhoe Bay, with meals. Four-hour tours of the oil fields round out the arrangement. It is also possible to take a one-day package tour, flying both ways between Fairbanks and Prudhoe Bay via the Inuit village of Utqiagvik (Barrow), the northernmost town in the United States.

The **Denali Highway** ⑮. The Denali Highway – not to be confused with the Denali Park Road – is a 135-mile (217km), mostly gravel route between the villages of Paxson and Cantwell. With constant views of the soaring Alaska range, this route makes for an impressive trip through some of Alaska's wildest countryside. Organized tours of this wildlife-rich corridor are available; some stop for a hearty meal at the friendly and atmospheric **Maclaren River Lodge**. Many see this route as a crowd-free alternative to the Denali Park Road.

Dawson City, Yukon, Canada. Just 60 miles (100km) or so over the border in Canada's Yukon Territory, **Dawson City** is the quintessential Gold Rush town. While Skagway served as a staging site for Klondike-bound prospectors, Dawson City, at the confluence of the Yukon and Klondike Rivers, was their destination.

Dawson City currently attracts more than 60,000 tourists a year with its historic gold rush theaters, bars, and brothels. Canada's first legalized casino, **Diamond Tooth Gertie's** (Sun-Wed 7pm–2am, Fri and Sat 2pm–2am; tel: 867-993 5525) – with a gold-rush era theme, and a Klondike-style dance revue are reminders that the Yukon was founded by hustlers, gold diggers, and dreamers, not fishermen or farmers. Literary buffs will want to visit the **Robert Service**, **Jack London** and **Frank Berton cabins**. The Robert Service cabin offers an especially good tour with poetry readings by Parks Canada actors.

The **Dawson City Museum** (mid-May to Labor Day daily 10am–6pm, Labor Day to Sep 15 Tue–Sat 10am–2pm; tel: 867-993 5291; charge; www.dawsonmuseum.ca) gives a good overview of the city's glory days, and a First Nations' viewpoint is available at the **Danoja Zho Cultural Centre** (Jun–Sep Mon–Sat 10am–5pm; tel: 867-993 6768; www.trondekheritage.com/danoja-zho), a community and heritage center for Tr'ondëk Hwëch'in (Klondike Gwichin) culture.

Note that passports are required to cross into Canada and return to the US.

TRAVEL TIPS

A SUMMARY OF PRACTICAL INFORMATION

CHOOSING A CRUISE

The first decision to make when choosing a cruise is how long a cruise do you want – or can you afford. Then you must consider what type would best suit you – a theme cruise, one packed with entertainment, a romantic sail, or one with lots of ports of call. Most people find that a 10-day cruise is ideal: one week for exploring both on- and offshore, with three days at sea.

TYPES OF CRUISE

Choosing a ship is a bit like buying a car. Big or small? Classic or modern? Luxurious or functional? Assess what you really want. The difference between so-called 'big ships' and 'small ships' could hardly be more stark, and it isn't simply a matter of tonnage or floor space. Thse days, large mainstream ships tend to be very large, indeed, carrying 3,000 passengers or more, soaring 14 stories above the water, and stretching to lengths of nearly 1,000ft (300m). By contrast, small ships in Alaska tend to be quite small, measuring around 100ft (30m) and carrying 12 to 140 passengers. Some are more like yachts, other have the utilitarian feel of expedition ships, and still others look like the miniaturized cruise ships that they really are.

Do your research. Each cruise line offers a different experience: the mega-ships of Carnival, Celebrity, Disney, Holland America, Norwegian, Princess, and Royal Caribbean provide the whole-big-ship experience – Broadway-style shows, diverse dining options, lots of deck sports and a high proportion of balcony cabins. Princess and Holland America also have their own shoreside hotels and rail cars which allow their passengers to stick with the same company during pre- and/or post-cruise travels. In contrast, a small or mid-sized ship, such as those belonging to Oceania, the smaller Holland America ships, or the upscale vessels of Regent, Seabourn or Silversea, will be more restful.

The smaller, often luxurious, ships can typically call in at tiny ports and villages along the Inside Passage, such as Petersburg or Kake, which are normally visited only by fishing boats and the private yachting set. These include Alaska Dream Cruises, American Cruise Lines, Discovery Voyages, Fantasy Cruises, Viking Cruises, Lindblad/National Geographic Cruises, and Un-Cruise Adventures.

Custom cruises that focus on individual itineraries and activities are offered by All Aboard Yacht Charters, environmentally-minded The Boat Company, Custom Alaska Cruises, and Sea Wolf Adventures. Sound Sailing operates Prince William Sound cruises in a sailboat while Maple Leaf Adventures offers the Inside Passage in a renovated tugboat and a 'tall-ship' schooner.

If you want to depart from the standard itineraries, opt for 'expedition' cruises offered by Windstar and Silversea, with trans-Pacific itineraries between Alaska and Russia or Japan, or one of several Northwest Passage cruises between Alaska and Greenland or New York, with stops in western Alaska ports of call. While these choices take you to the literal ends of the earth, the amenities (and prices) are always top notch.

Know your cruise lines and ships. Although cruise lines may sound similar in their advertisements, they offer different vacation experiences at different rates. Some specialize in great food, while others have a vast array of shipboard amenities, such as rock-climbing walls and full work-out facilities.

Once you've decided on a particular cruise line, remember that not all ships in a fleet offer the same standards. Newer ones tend to be more expensive, but come with the latest features and more cabins with balconies. Apart from the cruise line's website, a top source of information is the annual Berlitz Cruising and Cruise Ships guide, which provides exhaustive reviews of nearly 300 vessels.

Getting there. Once you've chosen your cruise, start looking for flights to and from your embarkation and disembarkation points. The most economical tickets are available through online ticket brokers such as www.orbitz.com, www.kayak.com, and a dozen others. Otherwise, speak with a travel agent, tourist board, airline, or your cruise operator to organize transportation to and from the embarkation and disembarkation points.

THEME CRUISES

Some cruises are designed around specific themes that cater for a range of interests. While they're more popular in warm-weather locales than on Alaska cruises, several smaller companies, such as Un-Cruise Adventures, have begun offering theme cruises focusing on photography, marine biology, wine and music, while Silversea runs cruises for bridge-players and several operators organize departures specifically designed for singles.

Otherwise, theme cruises are usually arranged by cruise organizers – individuals, small companies, special interest groups, and non-profit organizations working with cruise operators – and not the cruise companies themselves. In this sense, the ships are 'hired out' by the cruise lines to specific groups. Themes may range from culinary, health-oriented, martial arts, and musical cruises to ethnic, gay and lesbian, and hard-core boot camp fitness voyages.

CHOOSING A CABIN

Accommodations on board run the gamut from smallish, claustrophobic inside cabins to outside ones with private balconies, to palatial suites with butler service. Balcony cabins offer the pleasant option of landscape and wildlife viewing in the privacy of your own space, but if you're just as happy sharing the experience with strangers, you'll save money opting with a simple outside cabin with a porthole.

Before deciding on a cabin, however, envisage how you will be spending your time on board. If you love sightseeing, you may not need an expensive cabin, as you probably won't be spending much time in it. But if you think you'll be spending sea days eating, reading and napping in the privacy of your cabin or relaxing on your balcony, then you'd be advised to go for a larger, more pricey, and more comfortable cabin.

Usually, the newer the ship, the more spacious the cabin, and you will always have a private bathroom. Smaller cruise lines, sailboats and yachts lean toward tiny, serviceable staterooms. Older, larger ships also tend to have small cabins without balconies that encourage guests to get out and about on the ship.

Specific cabins can be pre-booked on all ships, although some cruise lines charge for this facility. On large ships, the least expensive cabins tend to be windowless rooms in the interior of the ship; for most people, it's worth paying a little extra for at least a small porthole onto the outside world.

CRUISING WITH CHILDREN

Teen discos, children-only swimming pools, 'Circus at Sea' lessons, and supervised, age-related activity programs have become an intrinsic part of modern megaship cruising. Carnival and Royal Caribbean have indoor and outdoor children's facilities on their biggest ships, with huge areas dedicated to youngsters.

The facilities on the large Disney ships are superb, with special adult-only areas for those who need a break from the kids, while Princess, Royal Caribbean and Norwegian Cruise Lines all have children's facilities and entertainment. Princess ships even offer a night nursery, providing free care for sleeping infants while the parents relax.

DISABLED TRAVELERS

Cruising can be an ideal vacation for travelers with disabilities. Wheelchair users will find that most ships provide a relaxing, sociable setting while visiting multiple destinations. Take the advice of a specialist cruise agent before booking; make sure they provide specific information about airport transfers, boarding the ship, facilities on board, and the cabin itself.

All new ships have cabins adapted to wheelchair users, although in varying degrees. If you're uncomfortable walking long distances, consult the deck plans online, and avoid the very biggest ships, as getting around with a cane or walker may well be exhausting.

Some of the best options are escorted Alaska cruise packages for wheelchair users, organized in the US by Accessible Journeys (tel: 610-521 0339; www.accessiblejourneys.com). For UK travelers, Accessible Travel (tel: 01452-729 739; www.accessibletravel.co.uk) will assist in finding cruises that meet individual travelers' needs.

Older cruise ships do not generally provide special accommodations for those with hearing difficulties. Similarly, there are typically no special facilities for visually impaired passengers, but newer ships do have signage in Braille – on lift buttons and cabin door numbers.

HOME PORTS

A growing number of travelers are choosing cruising because they prefer not to fly or to deal with the hassles that can be inherent in airports – or they just want to enjoy their journey from 'see' level.

US and Canadian travelers who would rather not fly have the option to drive or travel by either bus or train to Seattle, Vancouver, San Francisco, or Los Angeles, and then join their Alaska cruise. Note, however, that the majority of Gulf of Alaska crossings require a one-way flight to or from Anchorage, but it is also possible to opt for real adventure and cruise one-way to Seward or Whittier (the cruise ports for Anchorage) and ride the Alaska Marine Highway ferries in the opposite direction.

PREPARING FOR THE TRIP

Many cruise lines don't have in-house reservations agents but they will provide a toll-free number, mail, or email brochures, and put you in touch with a local representative. You can find a specialist travel agent in your area through Cruise Lines International Association in the US (www.cruising.org), the UK's branch of Cruise Lines International (www.cruiseexperts.org), or the Australasia branch (www.cruising.org.au).

BOOKING A CRUISE

Online

Reputable cruise-specific websites include www.choosingcruising.co.uk, www.cruises.com, www.cruisebrothers.com, www.cruise411.com, www.

cruisecompete.com, http://cruise-compare.com as well as www.cruise-critic.com.

Agents in the US

Cruise.com claims to be one of the largest websites specializing in cruises; tel: 888-333 3116; www.cruise.com.

Cruise Holidays has branches all over the US, Canada and the UK; tel: 866-336 1882; www.cruiseholidays.com.

Cruise Store, 55 Maple Street, East Longmeadow, MA 01028; tel: 800-732 2897; www.cruisestore.com. .

Liberty Travel has branches all over the US; tel: 888-271 1584; www.libertytravel.com.

Agents in the UK

The Cruise People, 88 York Street, London W1H 1QT; tel: 020 7723 2450; www.cruisepeople.co.uk.

TCCT Retail Ltd, The Thomas Cook Business Park, Coningsby Road, Peterborough PE3 8SB; tel: 01733 224 804; www.co-operativetravel.co.uk.

Ideal Cruising, Grosvenor House, Prospect Hill, Redditch, B97 4DL;tel: 0330 303 8331; www.cruise.co.uk.

Marion Owen Travel, 23 Portland Street, Hull, HU2 8JX; tel: 01482 212525; www.marionowentravel.com.

Mundy Cruising, 50-51 Wells Street, London W1T 3PP; tel: 020 7399 7670; www.mundycruising.co.uk.

Agents in Australia and New Zealand

Harvey World Travel; tel: 1-300 855 492; www.harveyworld.com.au.

ecruising.travel; Level 9, 64 Castlereagh Street, Sydney NSW 2000; tel: 1-300 369 848; www.ecruising.travel.

Cruise Centre; tel: 1-300 137 445; www.cruisecentre.com.au.

iCruise, 131 New North Road, Eden Terrace, Auckland 1145, NZ; tel: 0800 427 847; www.icruise.co.nz.

Agents in South Africa

Cruises-for-Africa, PO Box 37546, Valyland, Cape Town 7978; tel: 021 782-6979, www.cruises-for-africa.co.za.

COUNTING THE COST

Generally, your booking price will cover your cabin and food in the main dining room – but there are plenty of add-on costs.

Hidden extras. Items included in the price of the cruise: all food; all entertainment; use of the gym and sports facilities (but not always all of them); transfers from the port (usually); port taxes; room service (sometimes); shuttle buses into town (sometimes); flights (usually); use of the ship's self-service laundry (usually); use of the ship's library; the captain's cocktail party.

Items not included: alcoholic drinks (except on Silversea, Seabourn, and Regent Seven Seas); tips (unless stated); travel insurance; spa treatments; shore excursions; medical care; internet access and telephone calls from the satellite phone. Some cruise lines also charge extra for the following: visits to the bridge; use of some sports equipment; 'premium' exercise classes such as yoga; mineral water in cabins; room service; tea and coffee and shuttle buses. Most charge extra for dining in 'alternative' restaurants (ie not the main dining room).

Tipping. Tipping staff should be considered obligatory. On Silversea, Seabourn, and Regent Seven Seas, some or all of the tips are included in the price. Many lines, including Carnival, Disney and Royal Caribbean allow or even insist that all tips are pre-paid, while others automatically add a suggested amount to your onboard account, or place an envelope for cash in the cabin on the final evening.

HEALTH

Although medical assistance is available on board larger ships, it's wise to have a health check before traveling, and be sure to carry along any medications or supplements you'll be needing.

Drinking water. Drinking water provided on ships and all tap water in the US and Canada are considered safe to drink. Choose specific brands of bottled water, however, if you'd rather avoid tap water treated with chlorine and/or fluoride.

Health insurance. It must be noted that health care in the US is extremely expensive, which means that it's a very good idea for foreigners to have a good travel health insurance policy that is valid in the US. For Canada, reciprocal agreements may cover expenses for citizens of Commonwealth countries, but it may be more convenient to have a backup policy on hand.

Immunization. No immunizations are required for either Canada of the US, unless you're arriving from a region listed for a specific health risk. However, there's always a risk of minor injury, so you may wish to be up-to-date with tetanus immunization.

Insects. Mosquitoes, blackflies, horseflies, and 'no-see-ums' can all be a major nuisance in Alaska and Canada, but they do not carry disease. For the mosquitoes and flies, use a repellent containing at least 30 percent DEET. No-see-ums are best repelled with a product known as 'Skin-so-Soft', produced by Avon.

Sun protection. If you need sun protection on an Alaska cruise, count your blessings – but have it on hand, because there's a good chance that you will be blessed with at least a day or two of magical weather.

Hypothermia. The cold, rainy conditions that prevail along the Inside Passage increase the risk of hypothermia – that is, dangerous cooling of the body core – for those not dressed for the weather. The layering system, which allows for easy addition or removal of layers, works best. In extreme circumstances, such as walking on deck when the ship is underway, you should have streetwear on the bottom layer, followed by one or two insulating layers, then topped off – if necessary – with a waterproof layer.

PASSPORTS & VISAS

All passengers on an Alaska cruise need a passport except US citizens cruising from a US port to Alaska without stopping anywhere in Canada along the way. On the Alaska Marine Highway, even US citizens need a passport if their ferry stops in Prince Rupert, British Columbia, and Haines and Skagway, Alaska.

It is common practice for passengers to hand over their passport at check-in until the end of the cruise, so make a photocopy to leave at home and another for the trip. Anyone wishing to purchase alcohol in Alaska – or even visit a bar or a shop where alcohol is sold – will need to temporarily retrieve their passport from the purser.

Each passenger is given a cruise ship ID card, which is swiped and checked every time they leave the ship; on modern ships, it doubles as a room key and a charge card. This system also allows the ship to determine whether any passengers are missing when the ship is about to depart.

Visas and electronic authorizations. Visas are required by all visitors entering the US, unless they meet requirements for the US Visa Waiver Program, which is open to citizens of Australia, New Zealand, the UK, Ireland, Japan, South Korea, and most EU countries. Note that South Africans do require visas to enter the US. In addition, all foreigners flying into the US must obtain an Electronic System for Travel Authorization (ESTA) before arrival; for details, see https://esta.cbp.dhs.gov/esta. This includes citizens from all of the 38 countries that participate in the US Visa Waiver Program. The ESTA requires that you have more than six months before your passport expires and that you have a machine-readable passport with an embedded chip. The fee for ESTA is US$14 per person.

All foreigners traveling to or through Canada, except US citizens or permanent residents, must present a current passport (however, US citizens and permanent residents DO require a passport to re-enter the US from Canada). Citizens of most Commonwealth and EU countries, as well as Japan and South Korea, do not need visas to enter Canada, but South Africans do need a visa. Everyone entering the US from Canada, however briefly, will require a passport with at least six months' validity. Since March 2016, visa exempt travelers entering Canada by air need an ETA, or Electronic Travel Authorization; see www.cic.gc.ca/english/visit/eta-start.asp. For more information, call 204-983 3500 (outside Canada), 1-800-461 9999 (within Canada), or visit www.cbsa.gc.ca. Visitors may be asked to produce return tickets and possibly evidence that they have sufficient funds for their stay in Canada.

WHEN TO GO

Just before the first cruise ship arrives in Alaska, store merchants bring out colorful hanging flower baskets and the cities seem to 'bloom' overnight. Gift shops, which may have been closed over the winter, are re-opened, swept out, shelves stocked and windows polished. The main cruising season runs from June to mid-August, when the state boasts mild temperatures and, from South Central Alaska northward, seemingly endless daylight. During those times, all tours, parks, campgrounds, trains, buses, ferries, restaurants, hotels, B&Bs, and other service-related facilities are running at full speed.

Those looking to avoid the busiest times may want to choose a shoulder-season cruise. In May, which is typically the nicest month weather-wise, passengers typically experience fine weather, excellent whale-watching, and less crowded conditions in ports of call. Late season cruises from late August to mid-September will also avoid crowds, and in addition provide opportunities to see the aurora borealis and the autumn colors of the birch and tundra. The down side is that during shoulder seasons, favorite tourist destinations and on-shore transport, lodgings, restaurants and other amenities are more limited than in the height of summer.

Public holidays. In Alaska, public holidays include: New Year's Day (1 January), Independence Day (4 July), Alaska Day (18 October), Veteran's Day (11 November), and Christmas Day (25 December). Other public holidays, with varying dates (some due to Monday holiday adjustment), are Martin Luther King Day (January), President's Day (February), Seward's Day (March), Memorial Day (May), Labor Day (September), Columbus Day (October), and Thanksgiving Day (November).

Time zone. The entire state of Alaska (except some western islands) is on Alaska-Yukon time, which is GMT (UTC) minus nine hours. During Daylight Savings time, from early March to early November – when most cruising occurs – it's GMT (UTC) minus eight hours. The west coast of the US and Canada is on Pacific time, which is always one hour closer to GMT (UTC).

The Inside Passage climate. Southeast Alaska's temperate rainforest features a mild, wet, maritime climate. Summer temperatures average 51º to 65ºF (11º to 18ºC) in Ketchikan, at the southern end, and 47º to 60ºF (8º to 16ºC) around Yakutat (Hubbard Glacier), at the northern end. The entire Panhandle experiences heavy precipitation (13.5ft/4.1m per year average in Ketchikan; 11ft/3.3m around Hubbard Glacier), which creates the ideal environment for the area's unique flora and fauna.

For visitors, these conditions necessitate excellent protection from wind and rain. Plan to dress in layers and make sure the outermost layer is waterproof. A hooded rain jacket with a drawstring, a lightweight knitted hat, gloves, waterproof pants, and comfortable waterproof footwear are ideal. Umbrellas, on the other hand, are unwieldy and tend to turn inside out in wind gusts. Plus, locals don't use them, and visitors who do may find themselves the subject of local amusement.

WHAT TO BRING

On an Alaska cruise, you need to come prepared for any climatic eventuality. First, you'll need walking shoes, deck shoes, sunblock, mosquito repellent, seasickness remedies, a brimmed sun hat, rain gear, and thermal clothing layers, including a winter fleece, which will be useful on deck when the ship is underway. If your ship has a pool or spa, be sure to bring swimwear, and also have gymwear if you're up for onboard workouts. You'll also want to have binoculars for wildlife-viewing, memory cards for your camera, a phone charger, and any regular medication you need.

WHAT TO WEAR

On some ships, cruising in Alaska will mean bringing two separate wardrobes: one for the cruise and one for overland travel before or after.

On the ship. Some cruise lines, inspired by NCL's informal 'Freestyle' cruising, have done away with compulsory formal nights, although

Seabourn, Celebrity, Holland America, and some others do have gala nights. On these, a week's cruise will generally have one or two formal nights and a mixture of casual and informal dress codes on the other nights. If you're unsure, check with your chosen line to see what will be appropriate.

Casual: Smart casual wear, but no shorts or vests.

Informal: Trouser and a smart shirt/jacket for men; cocktail dresses for women.

Formal: Dinner jacket/tuxedo or dark suit for men; evening dress for women.

On shore. Alaskans are reknowned for their relaxed attitude toward life, and that extends to their fashion sense. In Alaskan ports of call, casual is the name of the game and anything not typically worn by a lumberjack or fisherman could be considered formal attire. As a rule of thumb, just about anything appropriate for the weather will be acceptable.

GETTING THERE

The hubs for Alaska cruising will be Seattle, Washington, USA; Vancouver, British Columbia, Canada; and Anchorage, Alaska, USA (for one-way southbound cruising), but an increasing number operate out of San Francisco and Los Angeles, California, USA.

The most economical way to find good value flights is online. The offer is vast and it's worth plodding through several sites, as each has deals with different airlines and fare differences between them can be substantial.

San Francisco and Los Angeles are world airline hubs served by numerous international airlines from London, as well as from other parts of Europe, Asia and Australasia. For travel to Vancouver or Seattle, and by extension, Anchorage, the following airlines offer direct or convenient one-stop service from the UK:

Air Canada (www.aircanada.com)

British Airways (www.britishairways.com)

Delta (www.delta.com)
Finnair (www.finnair.com)
Iberia (www.iberia.com)
Icelandair (www.icelandair.com)
KLM (www.klm.com)
Lufthansa (www.lufthansa.com)
United (www.united.com)
Virgin Atlantic (www.virginatlantic.com)
Airports.
Anchorage Ted Stevens International (ANC, http://www.dot.state.ak.us/anc/); three miles SW, taxi 15 min, US$20

London Heathrow, UK (LHR, www.heathrow.com), 15 miles W, Underground 25 minutes, £9.50 per person

Los Angeles International (LAX, www.lawa.org/welcome_lax.aspx) 10 miles SW, taxi 30 minutes, US$100; Uber 30 minutes, US$25; bus one hour, US$5 per person;

San Francisco International (SFO, www.flysfo.com) 20 miles S, taxi 45 minutes, US$60; BART train 20 minutes, US$8.95 per person

Seattle Sea-Tac International (SEA, www.portseattle.org/Sea-Tac/) 16 miles S, taxi 40 minutes, US$50

Vancouver International (YVR, www.yvr.ca) 15 km SW, taxi 30 minutes, C$35; Sky Train 30 minutes, C$8.75 per person

LIFE ON BOARD

Modern ships cater for every age, taste, and budget, with many new vessels that can each seem more innovative than the last.

ACTIVITIES AND ENTERTAINMENT

By design, most big ships are quite busy, with activities, entertainment, and meals programmed so that, if you cared to, you could be occupied during every waking moment on board. As such, they're ideal for families, allowing parents and children to pursue their own interests.

They're also the better choice for people who want to experience the wonders of Alaska, but realize that glaciers, whales, and mountains won't hold their attention every minute of the day.

If you want a show in the evening, multiple restaurants, sports options, and maybe a casino or a pool, choose one of the larger lines, such as Carnival, Royal Caribbean, Princess, or Norwegian. More refined entertainment is available on Holland America or Celebrity, and for refined entertainment plus enhanced service and facilities, go with Crystal or Regent.

After-dinner shows. The standard ship's evening entertainment, which could be stand-up comedy, a cabaret singer or a splashy Broadway-style show, includes two nightly performances, one after each dinner sitting.

Casinos. Gambling is a feature on most large ships and most casinos provide gaming lessons, as well as slot machines. Casinos operating in international waters on Alaska cruises tend to be more laid back than those in Las Vegas and elsewhere. Ships' casinos are closed one hour before arriving in port and one hour after leaving. They're also closed in National Park waters around Glacier Bay.

Big production shows. Big production shows can be spellbinding at sea, and some ships boast technical facilities that are superior to those in a top theater. Big-name musicals, futuristic circus shows, opera, and Las Vegas-style reviews may all be staged on ships.

Live music. Ships nowadays offer everything from concert pianists to scantily clad female string quartets. Some have great tribute bands, talented jazz musicians, and excellent orchestras. Occasionally, you'll also have big-name entertainment.

Nightclubs and discos. With mixed age groups to cater for, the resident DJs generally play it safe and include old favorites in their repertoire.

Religious services. Interdenominational Christian services are held on most cruise ships, conducted either by the captain or an on-board chaplain. Special Jewish charters will have a rabbi aboard.

Talks and lectures. Many ships have guest lecturers and guest speakers who discuss topics related to the region or a special interest group aboard. Through Glacier Bay, some ships have an on-board National Park ranger who provides natural history interpretation.

COMMUNICATION

Telephones. Making telephone calls using a ship's satellite system is expensive, at up to US$12 per minute. It is cheaper to make calls from a land line in port, or from a mobile phone with a roaming contract. All North American passengers with a roaming-enabled phone will receive a signal through much of Southeast Alaska. Note that connecting to Canadian cell towers will incur international roaming charges.

When out of range of land-based towers, service is provided by Wireless Maritime Services (WMS) called Cellular at Sea, which is switched on when the ship is more than 12 miles (19km) from land. Using Cellular at Sea, you're charged international roaming rates ranging from US$2 to US$6 per minute, depending on your carrier.

The international dialing code for the US and Canada is 1. Area codes are as follows: Alaska (907); Vancouver, BC (604); Victoria, BC (250) Seattle, WA (206); Bellingham, WA (360); San Francisco (415); and Los Angeles (213, 323, 310). To dial an international call from the US or Canada, dial (011) plus the country code, area code (minus any leading zeros), and local number.

Internet. Internet is available at shops and other businesses in all Alaskan ports of call. At sea, nearly all ships now offer satellite Wi-Fi, or hybrid satellite/land-based links. On some ships, Internet access can be as much as US$.45 to US$.75 per minute, or they may charge by the megabyte either piecemeal or in a package deal. Social media packages that exclude bandwidth hogs like Skype and Face-Time can be as little as US$5 per day, while a full Internet access package, when available, starts at around US$25 per device per day. Some upper-range lines, such as Oceania and Regent Seven Seas, provide free internet.

ETIQUETTE

Cruise lines are strict about the public areas being non-smoking, and some provide a cigar lounge for smokers.

For copyright reasons, it is forbidden to film or record any of the ship's entertainers.

If you're invited to dine with the captain, consider it an honor and reply immediately. Be sure to observe the dress code, which in this case will probably be considered formal.

For security, visits to the bridge are now rarely permitted, but small ships may still allow access.

FOOD AND DRINK

That you can eat around the clock on a cruise is no exaggeration, so unless you want to pack on some poundage, try to eat in moderation. Unless you dine in a 'specialty' restaurant on board, all meals on a cruise are included in the fare.

Bars. Ships' bars range from sophisticated lounges to Irish-themed pubs. All drinks purchased in the bar can be charged to your bill, but be aware that some ships will automatically add a 'gratuity' of 15–18 percent.

Coffee shops. Cappuccino and espresso from machines are usually better than cruise-ship tea and coffee. Afternoon tea is provided on many ships, with white-glove service, dainty cakes, and sandwiches.

Drinking water. Although it's considered safe to drink, the chlorinated water on cruise ships doesn't taste very good. Bottled water is available, but usually costs extra.

Dining and restaurants. Some ships offer from two to four different dinner sittings in the dining rooms, while others have 'open seating', meaning you eat when you like and sit where you like. Smaller ships, carrying fewer than 100 or so passengers, tend to have just one sitting where all the passengers dine together.

As well as a main dining room, many ships have specialty restaurants where a small premium is charged for a different menu and more exclusive surroundings. Vegetarians, vegans, and people with other dietary requirements are usually well catered for.

Room Service. Room service is usually included in the cost of the cruise, although some lower-budget cruise lines either charge for it or do not offer it. Many ships have tea- and coffee-making facilities in the individual cabins.

MONEY

Cruise operators encourage guests to register a credit card at the beginning of a voyage for on-board expenses. Otherwise, a bill will be compiled to be settled on the day of departure. While on board, whether a credit card is registered or not, everything is paid for using a special card issued by the ship.

Currency on board all Alaska cruise ships is the US dollar, and there is usually an ATM near the shops or casino. However, you'll pay a substantial ATM transaction fee and non-US banks will add a foreign currency exchange charge. There may be currency exchange for Canadian dollars at the ship's customer relations desk, but rates are not competitive, so carry an ATM card or be sure to have sufficient US dollars for any extra tipping or necessary cash purchases. When the US dollar is higher than the Canadian dollar, US dollars are usually accepted at Canadian ports of call at a 1:1 ratio, but change will be given in Canadian dollars.

SHIP FACILITIES

Medical care. All cruise ships have a doctor and nurse on board (the exception being cargo ships, or private ships). Facilities vary but a ship's doctor should be able to treat most ailments. Seriously ill passengers may be stabilized until the ship arrives in port, or is airlifted off. There is a fee for consulting the ship's doctor.

Norovirus, a common gastro-intestinal virus, occurs on cruise ships, as it does in hospitals and hotels, and it can spread quickly. If you have diarrhea, vomiting, and fever, report to the ship's doctor immediately. Avoid the virus by using the antiseptic hand wipes that are distributed on board and by washing hands scrupulously.

Cinema and TV. All ships offer in-cabin TV, usually showing satellite channels, movies, and the ship's channels. Many ships have a cinema, too, showing first-run movies.

Gentlemen hosts. A 'gentleman host', also known as a dance host, is a feature on traditional cruises with Crystal, Cunard, Silversea, and Holland America. Personable single men in their 50s and 60s are employed to act as dancing and dinner hosts for unaccompanied older women.

Library. The ship's library provides a quiet retreat and an endless source of free reading material, from novels to guidebooks.

The purser. The Purser's Office (also called Reception, Guest Relations, or the Information Desk) is the nerve center of the ship for general passenger information and minor problems. This is the place to pick up DVDs, ship-compiled newspapers, and the ship's program.

Spas. Sea spas now rival land-based health facilities in terms of the services offered. You can treat yourself to facials and massages, have your teeth whitened, consult an acupuncturist or have a Botox treatment. US$120 for a facial, a 55-minute massage, or a reflexology session. Book ahead for treatments on sea days, as they are very popular.

Water sports. Alaska cruises aren't specifically known for water sports, but the large ships have swimming pools as well as very welcoming hot tubs to warm your bones. Many ports do offer shore excursions that include kayaking lessons or short kayak adventures through sheltered waters that are rich in marine life.

LIFE ON SHORE

Aboard the ship, you're enjoying an exhilarating international environment, but on shore, you're in Alaska, where ports typically operate at very low stress levels, even with five cruise ships in port. Thanks to politics, Juneau, which is Alaska's capital city, is probably the least relaxed, while Ketchikan, Sitka, Skagway, and Seward are in fact just small towns that function at a lethargic small town pace.

SHORE EXCURSIONS

Although they can be expensive, shore excursions tend to get snapped up quickly. You can often book them at the same time as buying your cruise, but take care not to book too many tours. A crowded schedule can be punishing on the pocket, as well as physically strenuous.

Assembly times can be as early as 5am and may entail bus travel and only a short time at each sight of interest, so choose them carefully. Practically all shore excursions factor in some souvenir shopping time. **Independent shore tours**. You can see and do what you want if you're prepared to organize your own excursion, and it's often cheaper than a cruise-line tour. However, time is usually limited in port, so you need to research the port of call first, bring a good map or GPS, and check that the transport times coincide with the ship's arrival and departure. The good news is that lots of local tour companies offer excursions with cruise ship passengers in mind and are fastidious about accommodating the ships' schedules. But if you're late returning, the ship won't wait unless you're on a ship-organized tour, and it's your responsibility to catch up with the ship at the next port.

CRUISE LINE INFORMATION

CRUISE COMPANIES

Alaska Dream US: 1512 Sawmill Creek Road, Sitka, AK 99835; tel: 907-747 8100; www.alaskadreamcruises.com. Intimate small-boat cruises around Southeast Alaska, emphasising wildlife-viewing and Native culture.

All-Aboard Yacht Charters US: #436, 310 E Dalby Road, Union, WA 98582; tel: 800-767 1024; www.alaskacharters.com. Informal small-yacht cruising in Southeast Alaska, focusing on wildlife-viewing and a sense of adventure.

American Cruise Lines US: 741 Boston Post Road, Suite 200, Guilford, CT 06437; tel: 800-460-4518. UK: tel: 0808-101 2713; www.american cruiselines.com. Small-boat cruising from Seattle area to small ports in Southeast Alaska.

Boat Company US: PO Box 1839, Poulsbo, WA 98370; tel: 360-697 4242; www.theboatcompany.org. Small-ship cruising in Southeast Alaska.

Carnival Cruise Lines, US: 3655 NW 87th Avenue, Miami, FL 33178; tel: 800-764 7419. UK: Carnival House, 5 Gainsford St, London SE1 2NE; tel: 0843-374 2272; www.carnival.com. Big ships, budget prices, and emphasis on fun. Popular with singles and youthful clients.

Celebrity US: 1050 Caribbean Way, Miami, FL 33132; tel: 800-647 2251; www.celebritycruise.com. UK: The Heights, Brooklands, Weybridge KT13 0NY; tel: 0844-493 2043; www.celebritycruises.co.uk. Larger mid-size ships, leaning toward the luxury side.

Clipper Cruises US: 11969 Westline Industrial Drive, St Louis, MO 63146; tel: 800-325 0010; www.clippercruise.com. Small-ship, upmarket cruising with emphasis on informal, educational and personable cruising. The Bering Sea and Inside Passage itineraries feature offbeat ports of call.

Crystal US: 2049 Century Park East, Suite 1400, Los Angeles, CA 90067; tel: 800-446 6620; www.crystalcruises.com. Smaller mid-sized ships with a focus on service and luxury. Sails from San Francisco.

Cunard, US: 24305 Town Center Drive, Suite 200, Valencia, CA 91355; tel: 800-728 6273. UK: Carnival House, 100 Harbour Parade, Southampton SO15 1 ST; tel: 0843-373 1000; www.cunard.com. Luxury-oriented Cunard offers a trans-Pacific cruise between Japan and Vancouver via Alaska.

Custom Alaska Cruises US: 804 3rd Street, Douglas, AK; tel: 970-217 6359; www.sikumi.com. Hire the entire small 12-passenger ship for custom private cruising through the Inside Passage, beginning in tiny Petersburg, Alaska.

Discovery Voyages US: 1 Harborview Drive, Whittier, AK 99693; tel: 800-324 7602; www.discoveryvoyages.com. Small-boat cruising on Prince William Sound on a 65ft- (20m-) yacht.

Disney US: Guest Communications, PO Box 10238, Lake Buena Vista, FL 32830; tel: 800-951 3532; https://disneycruise.disney.go.com. Well-appointed mega-ship cruising with emphasis on entertainment, including kid-oriented features; popular with families.

Fantasy Cruises US: PO Box 448, Pierson, FL 32180; tel: 800-234 3861; www.smallalaskaship.com. Small-ship cruises between Seattle and Juneau or within the Inside Passage. Flexible itineraries, adventurous excursions, and environmentally-minded approach.

Holland America US: 300 Elliott Avenue West, Seattle, WA 98119; tel: 877-932 4259. UK: Carnival House, 100 Harbour Parade, Southampton SO15 1 ST; tel: 0843-374 2300; www.hollandamerica.com. Well-established in the market and popular with middle-aged and older clients, it uses large ships and operates stress-free pre- and post-cruise itineraries.

Lindblad Expeditions/National Geographic US: 96 Morton Street, 9th Floor, New York, NY 10014; tel: 212-261 9081; www.expeditions.com. Small ships with an informal atmosphere and a focus on educational activities and shore excursions in wilderness locations or small ports of call. Attracts mainly active, older, well-traveled clients.

Maple Leaf Adventures Canada: 1110 Government Street #209, Victoria, BC V82 1Y2; tel: 250-386 7245; www.mapleleafadventures.com. Small-ship boutique cruising in British Columbia and Alaska.

Norwegian US: 1509 North Cruise Boulevard, Miami, FL 33132; tel: 305-372 9902. UK: Mountbatten House, Grosvenor Square, Southampton SO15 2RP; tel: 0800-040 1182; www.ncl.com. Large to mega-ships; activity-oriented but with a relaxed and informal atmosphere.

Oceania Inside Passage cruises between San Francisco, Seattle, and Vancouver on luxury, mid-size ships. Emphasis on lectures, courses, and self-improvement.

Ponant US: 420 Lexington Avenue, Suite 2838, New York, NY 10170; tel: 888-400 1082; https://us.ponant.com. Luxury large-yacht cruising with a French flair.

Princess The most ubiquitous in the Alaska market, priced in the mid-range with large to mega-ships; operates extensive pre- and post-cruise itineraries, popular with middle-aged to older clients.

Regent Seven Seas US: 8300 NW 33rd Street, Suite 100, Miami, FL 33122; tel: 844-473 4368. UK: Beresford House, Town Quay, Southampton SO14 2AQ; tel: 02380-682 280; www.rssc.com. Elegant cruising in mid-sized ships, with fine dining, a tasteful, relaxed atmosphere, and shore excursions included; mainly Inside Passage cruising, plus an occasional Northwest Passage crossing.

Royal Caribbean US: 1050 Caribbean Way, Miami, FL 33132; tel: 800-398 9819. UK: Building 3, The Heights, Weybridge KT13 0NY; tel: 0844-493 4005. Australia: Level 2, 80 Arthur Street, North Sydney NSW 2060; tel: 02-4331 5400; www.royalcaribbean.com. Mega-ships ply the Inside Passage round-trip from Vancouver or one-way between Vancouver and Seward; expect relatively informal style with tasteful décor and just a hint of elegance.

Seabourn US: 300 Elliott Avenue West, Seattle, WA 98119; tel: 206-626 9179. UK: Carnival House, 100 Harbour Parade, Southampton SO15 1 ST; tel: 0843-373 2000; www.seabourn.com. They cultivate an intimate and luxurious ambience with smaller mid-sized ships, gourmet meals, open bars, no tipping, and unique Inside Passage itineraries including ports on the British Columbia coast.

Silversea US: 333 Avenue of the Americas, Suite 2600, Miami, FL 33131; tel: 888-978 4070. UK: Level 3, The Asticus Building, 21 Palmer Street, London SW1H 0AD; tel: 0844-251 0837; www.silversea.com. Luxury cruising on mid-size ships between Vancouver and Seward, plus trans-Pacific to Japan and a unique itinerary between Nome, Alaska, and Wrangel Island, Russia.

Un-Cruise Adventures US: 3826 18th Avenue West, Seattle, WA 98119; tel: 888-862 8881; www.uncruise.com. The ultimate small-ship adventure option through the Inside Passage; explores every corner of Southeast Alaska. The focus is on active excursions, including kayaking, hiking, and wildlife-viewing.

Viking US: 5700 Canoga Avenue, Woodland Hills, CA 91367; tel: 866-984 5464; www.vikingcruises.com. Mid-sized ships and a bit of luxury, 11 days sailing one-way between Vancouver and Seward, with pre- and post-cruise programs available. Currently the only line that calls in at Valdez, Alaska.

Windstar US: 2101 4th Avenue Suite 210, Seattle, WA 98121; tel: 206-733 2703; www.windstarcruises.com. Inside Passage and trans-Pacific cruises, including the Aleutian Islands, on small 200 to 300 passenger yachts or motor-sailers. Several non-standard itineraries.

TOURIST INFORMATION

Alaska Public Lands Information Centers 605 W 4th Avenue, Anchorage, AK 99501; tel: 907-644 3661; anch_web_mail@nps.gov; www.alaskacenters.gov

Anchorage Convention and Visitors' Bureau 524 W 4th Avenue, Anchorage, AK 99501; tel: 907-276 4118; www.anchorage.net

Astoria Warrenton Chamber of Commerce 111 West Marine Drive, Astoria, OR 97103; tel: 503-325-6311; visitors@oldoregon.com; www.travelastoria.com

British Columbia www.hellobc.com

California 555 Capitol Mall Suite 1100, Sacramento, CA 95814; tel: 877-225 4367; www.visitcalifornia.com

Denali National Park Visitor Access Center PO Box 9, Denali Park, AK 99755; tel: 907-683 9532; www.nps.gov/dena

Fairbanks Convention and Visitors' Bureau 101 Dunkel Street Suite 111, Fairbanks, AK 99701; tel: 907-456 5774; info@explorefairbanks.com; www.explorefairbanks.com

Juneau Convention and Visitors' Bureau 800 Glacier Avenue, Suite 101, Juneau, AK 99801; tel: 907-586 2201; info@traveljuneau.com; www.traveljuneau.com

Ketchikan Visitor Information Center 50 Front Street Suite 203, Ketchikan, AK 99901; tel: 907-225 6166; info@visit-ketchikan.com; www.visit-ketchikan.com

Kodiak Island Convention and Visitors' Bureau 100 Marine Way Suite 200, Kodiak, AK 99615; tel: 907-486 4782; www.kodiak.org

Los Angeles 6801 Hollywood Boulevard, Los Angeles, CA 90028; tel: 323-467 6412; www.discoverlosangeles.com

Mat-Su Convention and Visitors' Bureau 610 South Bailey Street, Palmer, AK 99645; tel: 907-746 5000; www.alaskavisit.com

Nome Convention and Visitors' Bureau 301 Front Street, Nome, AK 99762; tel: 907-443 6555; www.visitnomealaska.com

Petersburg Visitor Information Center 19 Fram Street, Petersburg, AK 99833; tel: 907-772 4636; www.petersburg.org

Prince of Wales Island Chamber of Commerce PO Box 490, Klawock, AK; tel: 907-755 2626; email: info@princeofwalescoc.org; www.prince ofwalescoc.org

San Francisco Pier 39 Building B Level 2, San Francisco, CA 94133; tel: 415-391 2000; vic1@sftravel.com; www.sftravel.com

Seattle 701 Pike Street Suite 100, Seattle, WA 98101; tel: 206-461 5840; visinfo@visitseattle.org; www.visitseattle.org

Seward/Kenai Fjords 1212 4th Avenue, Seward, AK 99664; tel: 907-422 0535; www.nps.gov/kefj

Sitka Convention and Visitors' Bureau 104 Lake Street, Sitka, AK 99835; tel: 907-747 8604; scvb@sitka.org; www.sitka.org

Skagway Convention and Visitors' Bureau 245 Broadway, Skagway, AK 99840; tel: 907-983 2854; skagwayinfo@skagway.org; www.skagway. com

Wrangell Visitor Center 293 Campbell Drive, Wrangell, AK 99929; tel: 907-874 2829; wrangell@wrangell.com; www.wrangell.com

Unalaska/Dutch Harbor Convention and Visitors' Bureau PO Box 545, Unalaska, AK 99685; tel. 907-581-2612; unalaskacvb@gmail.com; www. unalaska.info

Vancouver 20 Burrard Street, Vancouver, BC V6C 3L6; tel: 604-682 2222; visitvancouver@tourismvancouver.com; www.tourismvancouver.com

Victoria 812 Wharf Street, Victoria, BC V8W 1T3; tel: 250-953 2033; info@tourismvictoria.com; www.tourismvictoria.com

Washington (State) tel: 800-544 1800; tourisminfo@watourismalliance. com; www.experiencewa.com

INDEX

INSIGHT GUIDES POCKET GUIDE
ALASKA PORTS OF CALL

First Edition 2018

Editor: Carine Tracanelli
Author: Deanna Swaney
Head of Production: Rebeka Davies
Picture Editor: Tom Smyth
Cartography Update: Carte
Photography Credits: Alamy 25; Dan Joling/AP/REX/Shutterstock 5T; Denise Ferree/Chena Hot Springs Resort 108; Dreamstime 106, 113; Fotolia 4MC; Getty Images 1, 19, 50, 52, 65, 70, 74, 90, 92; iStock 4TC, 5M, 5M, 6L, 20, 29, 30, 34, 37, 38, 40, 43, 49, 54, 58, 66, 72, 84, 104; Matt Hage/Alyeska Resort 5BR; Photoshot 96; Princess Cruises 7R, 26, 62; Public domain 68; Robert Harding 4ML, 4TL, 5MC, 7, 57, 61; Shutterstock 5TC, 6R, 12, 14, 17, 22, 33, 44, 47, 76, 81, 82, 86, 89, 95, 98, 100, 103, 110, 114; SuperStock 11, 79
Cover Picture: iStock

Distribution
UK, Ireland and Europe: Apa Publications (UK) Ltd; sales@insightguides.com
United States and Canada: Ingram Publisher Services; ips@ingramcontent.com
Australia and New Zealand: Woodslane; info@woodslane.com.au
Southeast Asia: Apa Publications (SN) Pte; singaporeoffice@insightguides.com
Worldwide: Apa Publications (UK) Ltd; sales@insightguides.com

Special Sales, Content Licensing and CoPublishing
Insight Guides can be purchased in bulk quantities at discounted prices. We can create special editions, personalised jackets and corporate imprints tailored to your needs. sales@insightguides.com; www.insightguides.biz

All Rights Reserved
© 2018 Apa Digital (CH) AG and Apa Publications (UK) Ltd

Printed in China by CTPS

No part of this book may be reproduced, stored in a retrieval system or transmitted in any form or means electronic, mechanical, photocopying, recording or otherwise, without prior written permission from Apa Publications.

Contact us
Every effort has been made to provide accurate information in this publication, but changes are inevitable. The publisher cannot be responsible for any resulting loss, inconvenience or injury. We would appreciate it if readers would call our attention to any errors or outdated information. We also welcome your suggestions; please contact us at: hello@insightguides.com
www.insightguides.com